AUTHORS'
INSIGHTS

AUTHORS' INSIGHTS
TURNING TEENAGERS INTO READERS AND WRITERS

EDITED BY
DONALD R. GALLO

BOYNTON/COOK PUBLISHERS
HEINEMANN
PORTSMOUTH, NH

Boynton/Cook Publishers, Inc.
A subsidiary of Reed Elsevier Inc.
361 Hanover Street, Portsmouth, NH 03801-3912
Offices and agents throughout the world

The following have generously given permission to use quotations from
copyrighted works:

Pages 34–35: From *Running Loose* by Chris Crutcher. Copyright © 1983 by
Chris Crutcher. Reprinted by permission of William Morrow and Co., Inc.

Page 35: From *The Crazy Horse Electric Game* by Chris Crutcher. Copyright
© 1987 by Chris Crutcher. Reprinted by permission of William Morrow and Co., Inc.

Page 98: Poem by Carrie Orapello. Reprinted by permission of Marybeth Orapello.

Library of Congress Cataloging-in-Publication Data
Authors' insights : turning teenagers into readers and writers /
    edited by Donald R. Gallo.
        p.   cm.
    ISBN 0-86709-294-7
    1. Literature—Study and teaching (Secondary)   I. Gallo, Donald R.
PN59.A87   1991
807.1'2—dc20   91-34074
                                                                            CIP

Front-cover photo credits:
Sandy Asher by Jim Mayfield; Robert Cormier by Beth Bergman, Sentinel/Enterprise;
Paul B. Janeczko by Nadine Edris; Norma Fox Mazer by Ruth Putter; Richard Peck by
Don Lewis Photography; William Sleator by Dr. Esther K. Sleator

Cover design by Joni Doherty.
Designed by Hunter Graphics.
Printed in the United States of America.
95 96   9 8 7 6 5 4 3

Contents

The Contributors

Sandy Asher, currently writer-in-residence at Drury College in Springfield, Missouri, is the author of numerous short stories, poems, plays, and novels for young adults, including *Daughters of the Law, Things Are Seldom What They Seem,* and *Everything Is Not Enough.* For budding authors she has written *Where Do You Get Your Ideas?* and *Wild Words . . . and How to Train Them to Tell Stories.*

Robin F. Brancato teaches creative writing at Teaneck High School in New Jersey while working on her next novel. Brancato's highly-praised novels for teenagers include *Winning, Come Alive at 505, Sweet Bells Jangled Out of Tune, Facing Up, Uneasy Money,* and *Blinded by the Light,* which was made into a CBS Television Movie of the Week.

Robert Cormier, after a career as a newspaper reporter and editor, became one of the nation's most respected—and controversial— authors of novels for young adults with the publication of *The Chocolate War.* That was followed by *I Am the Cheese, After the First Death, The Bumblebee Flies Anyway, Beyond the Chocolate War,* and the frightening *Fade.* His most recent novels are the very touching *Other Bells for Us to Ring* and *We All Fall Down.* In early 1991 Robert Cormier received the Author Achievement Award presented jointly by the Young Adult Services Division of the American Library Association and *School Library Journal.*

Chris Crutcher has managed to find time away from his job as a child and family therapist working with child-abuse cases to write four hard-hitting, award-winning novels that combine sports themes with sensitive and humorous portrayals of teenage conflicts, starting with *Running Loose* and *Stotan!* and continuing with *The Crazy Horse Electric Game* and *Chinese Handcuffs*. His latest publication is a collection of short stories with sports themes entitled *Athletic Shorts*.

Paul B. Janeczko is a former high school English teacher, a poet, and the most productive anthologist of poems for young adults in the country. His collections include *Postcard Poems*; *Strings: A Gathering of Family Poems*; *Don't Forget to Fly*; *Poetspeak: In Their Work, About Their Work*; and *The Place My Words Are Looking For*. His latest collection, poems of adolescence, is *Preposterous!*

Harry Mazer has been writing young adult novels for over twenty years, two of them with his wife Norma, the first of which was *The Solid Gold Kid*. Among his much-liked novels are *Snowbound*, *The Last Mission*, *The Island Keeper*, *I Love You, Stupid!*, *When the Phone Rang*, *The Girl of His Dreams*, *City Light*, and his most recent, *Someone's Mother Is Missing*. The Mazers are currently collaborating on a third novel in which the teenagers' lives seem to them like a soap opera.

Norma Fox Mazer has published over twenty books, including two short-story collections as well as two novels written with her husband Harry, the most recent of which is *Heartbeat*. Among her award-winning novels for teenagers are *Up in Seth's Room*, *Taking Terri Mueller*, *Downtown*, *After the Rain*, *Silver*, and *Babyface*, along with the "name books" starting with *A, My Name Is Amy*, the most recent of which is *D, My Name Is Danita*.

Gloria D. Miklowitz has written novels that examine teenage encounters with rape (*Did You Hear What Happened to Andrea?*), child abuse (*Secrets Not Meant to be Kept*), AIDS (*Goodbye Tomorrow*), suicide (*Close to the Edge*), racism (*The War Between the Classes*), and nuclear devastation (*After the Bomb*). Three of her books have been made into award-winning television school-break specials. Her most recent novels are *Suddenly Super Rich*; *Anything to Win*; *Standing Tall, Looking Good*; and *You'll Never Make It to the Prom*.

Walter Dean Myers, born in West Virginia and raised in Harlem, has written a number of award-winning novels for teenagers, including *Fast Sam, Cool Clyde, and Stuff*; *It Ain't All for Nothin'*; *The*

Young Landlords; Crystal; Sweet Illusions; Hoops; and *Scorpions,* a Newbery Honor Book. For *Fallen Angels,* his highly acclaimed novel about the Vietnam War, Myers received the Coretta Scott King Award. His most recent novels are *Me, Mop, and the Moondance Kid* and *The Mouse Rap.*

Richard Peck, a former high school English teacher, in 1990 became the second person to receive the Author Achievement Award given jointly by *School Library Journal* and the Young Adult Services Division of the American Library Association. In addition to his essays, poems, short stories, and anthologies, he is best known for his witty and insightful views of the teenage world in his novels, most notably in *Are You in the House Alone?, Father Figure, Secrets of the Shopping Mall, Remembering the Good Times, Princess Ashley,* and the Blossom Culp series, especially *Ghosts I Have Been.* His most recent young adult novels are *Those Summer Girls I Never Met* and *Voices After Midnight.*

William Sleator gave up his job as rehearsal pianist for the Boston Ballet company and became a full-time writer, mostly of science fiction. *House of Stairs,* published in 1974, remains one of his most popular novels for teenagers but is being quickly equalled by *Interstellar Pig, Singularity, The Boy Who Reversed Himself, The Duplicate,* and *Strange Attractors.* Although Sleator makes his home in Boston, he spent most of 1991 living in Bangkok, Thailand. *The Spirit House* is his most recent publication.

Todd Strasser has published a dozen novels for young adults about various topics, including drugs (*Angel Dust Blues*), death (*Friends Till the End*), music (*Rock 'N' Roll Nights*), sexual responsibility (*A Very Touchy Subject*), computers (*The Complete Computer Popularity Program*), drunk driving (*The Accident*), and underwater treasure hunting (*Beyond the Reef*). He has also done the novelization of several popular films, including *The Wave, Ferris Bueller's Day Off,* and *Home Alone.*

The Editor

Donald R. Gallo is the author of *Presenting Richard Peck* and the editor of three anthologies of short stories for young adults—*Sixteen,*

Visions, and *Connections*; a collection of one-act plays for young adults—*Center Stage*; and a book of autobiographies of eighty-seven authors who write for young adults—*Speaking for Ourselves*. He is also a professor of English at Central Connecticut State University where he supervises student teachers and teaches courses in writing and in literature for young adults.

Introduction

During an interview I conducted with author Richard Peck in December of 1987, he pointed out that all of the important texts available on the subject of teaching literature to teenagers have been written by teachers and university professors. Although the views presented in those texts, such as *Literature for Today's Young Adults* by Kenneth Donelson and Alleen Nilsen, are excellent ones, they are the views mainly of educators, with only brief comments by well-known authors.

In addition, E.D. Hirsch and other contemporary scholars, along with former U.S. Secretary of Education William Bennett, forcefully publicized their own opinions during the 1980s about what teenagers should know in order to be considered educated and literate. (See, for example, E.D. Hirsch's *Cultural Literacy* or Diane Ravitch and Chester Finn's *What Do Our 17-Year-Olds Know?*) Their opinions generated much discussion and several proposals for revamping the core literature curricula at all levels from elementary through college.

No one asked the opinions of the writers who create many of the novels, short stories, and poems that are taught in middle, junior, and senior high schools across the nation or that are read independently by today's students. More specifically, as Richard Peck noted, no one has sought the opinions of that select group of contemporary writers of fiction who focus on teenagers as their main audience. Although many of them have strong and worthwhile opinions that they have expressed at professional conferences and in private about how literature and writing should be taught in schools, few of their individual opinions have been published for a wide audience, and none have been published collectively. Until now. These authors deserve to be heard.

The opinions in this book come from some of the foremost writers in the field of literature for young adults. Individually these writers have won a variety of awards—including a Newbery Honor Book Award, two Edgar Allan Poe Awards, a Coretta Scott King Award, two ALAN Awards, and two Author Achievement Awards—and nearly three dozen of their books have been named Best Books for Young Adults by the American Library Association. The works of nine of the contributors, in fact, appear on "The Best of the Best Books 1966–86" list chosen by the Young Adult Services Division of the American Library Association. Three of the authors were previously full-time English teachers, and those three plus two others currently teach writing on a part-time basis in public schools or conduct writing workshops outside of traditional school settings. All of these authors, as well as myself, have published books that are used as required or supplementary reading texts in various middle, junior, and senior high schools throughout the country.

When these distinguished authors were invited to share their experiences and express their opinions for this book, no restrictions were placed on what they should say. My only concern was that some of the authors might advocate teaching practices that run counter to contemporary theories or research findings. Although astute readers will come across occasional exceptions—for example, memorizing required vocabulary lists—almost every procedure advocated in these essays is surprisingly consistent with accepted practices of good teaching.

The chapters in this book are grouped into two basic categories: teaching literature and teaching writing, with two tangential but related chapters, one on book censorship and one on bringing authors into school classrooms. Harry Mazer sets the tone and direction for the book in the first chapter by describing the perception of literature he had as a teenager and what effects that had on his writing. To the young Harry, classics created the delusion that writing had to be perfect and that literature was something formidable, difficult, and sometimes unfathomable. He recommends that teachers use more readable books in their classrooms, books that "enchant and inform and move kids to want more."

Both Sandy Asher and Norma Fox Mazer mirror Harry Mazer's

perspective with insights from their own histories. Sandy Asher makes thought-provoking recommendations for discussing books used for in-common classroom reading, reinforcing reader response theorists by saying: "Every reader's response *matters*." Then, beginning with the assertion that "the way we love ice cream is the way we should love reading," Norma Fox Mazer goes on to make a case for what teachers should be doing to help students develop positive and rewarding reading habits.

Chris Crutcher, a therapist by training, looks at the healing effects of literature by noting how characters in his books gain insights into their troubled lives and how readers have been able to deal with pain in their own lives because of the connections they have made with the characters in books.

William Sleator then makes a strong case for using science fiction in secondary school classrooms, urging teachers to overcome their ignorance and contempt for it by noting the intellectual as well as the entertainment values of the genre. Good science fiction, Sleator asserts, as he recommends several specific titles, enables us to "look with special insight at our own lives and society."

Poetry, probably the most neglected of all the literary genres examined in secondary schools, has one of its most enthusiastic champions in Paul Janeczko, whose essay attempts to remove some of the mystery of poetry and recommends ways for teachers to choose and teach poems that will help students connect with those poems.

Next, Robert Cormier, one of the most highly regarded and most censored writers in the field of young adult books, describes how repeated attempts to remove and keep his novels out of junior and senior high school classrooms affect teenagers as well as his own perspective on writing.

The book then shifts to several articles about teaching writing, beginning with Richard Peck's penetrating comments about student writing achievement. Peck concludes his essay with eight pieces of advice to student writers, including his favorite dictum: "Never write what you know. Write what you can find out."

Then three authors describe specific workshop and classroom procedures they have used successfully to teach writing to contemporary students. Robin Brancato, using examples from her own fiction as well as from classical novels and poems, outlines a semester-long creative writing course in which she serves as motivator, coach, resource, and sympathetic evaluator. Next, Todd

Strasser, admitting that there is no one way to teach writing, provides the specific steps he follows, and some of the writing exercises
he uses, to teach a fiction writing workshop as he travels around
the country. Then Walter Dean Myers explains and illustrates how,
in a large city school, he leads young writers through the entire
writing process, from conception to publication, using his own
experiences as examples for the students.

The book concludes with Gloria Miklowitz's experienced recommendations for arranging an author's visit to a school and what
to do when he or she arrives. She includes advice on choosing an
author, contacting that person, planning the visit, financing it,
arranging the schedule, preparing the students and the faculty,
introducing the author, managing the daily activities, asking questions, and following up the visit.

Although these essays are by no means intended to provide
definitive methods for turning teenagers into readers and writers,
the wealth of informed experiences from which they come provide
educators with sensible, thought-provoking advice we dare not ignore.

I only became a writer when I finally said to myself: Damn the classics, damn the great writers, damn the delusion that what you write has to be perfect.

Big Books, Sex, and the Classics
Some Thoughts on Teaching Literature

Harry Mazer

YOU spend your life trying to figure out what's hokey and what's real, what's genuine and what's bullshit. That's the way I feel when I start talking literature. I mean the Great Books. The Classics. The Seventy-Six Greatest Authors of the Western World. Why not eighty-seven? Why not ninety-six? Who came up with this number? When we talk about the classics the garbage is piled so high it's hard to sort it all out. Why do we feel guilty when we don't teach classic literature? Why do we feel virtuous when we do? Why, when our leaders want to beat us down, do they demand a return to the classics? What is the hold of the classics?

We feel guilty if we can't identify Iago or discuss the symbolism of the White Whale. Guilty when we don't know the references and proud when we do. What's the big deal if you know that Nathaniel Hawthorne wrote *The Scarlet Letter*? It's helpful if you're addicted to crossword puzzles, and it's nice when you're reading an article or a review by a professor in the *New York Times*. But does it signify? Are you a donkey because you don't know Emerson's essay "Self-Reliance"?

When you call a literary work a classic it becomes a standard against which other literature is measured. It's writing, but not ordinary writing, and it's rarely contemporary. According to the well-placed and articulate priesthood of the classics, little of the contemporary literary outpouring is "literature." Rarely is a classic found in a magazine article or short story or the poetry tucked between the ads; or in the romances, historical novels and fantasies, mysteries, science fiction, children's books and young adult novels. Contemporary writings are too new, untested; they haven't survived the test of time. Their newness disqualifies them. The classics and the past go together like a dancing couple.

Classic, literary, genre, comic, adventure, mystery, juvenile, young adult: the hierarchies we set up make me fear for literature and reading. It's our snobbishness I fear, the divisions we make, the bins we put books in. The way we judge and set one book against another. Classics versus nonclassics. Good books versus bad books. If a book makes a reader want to read, can it be a bad book?

Classics are looked on as "better," "deeper," more "profound." They are said to contain truths that other writings don't, or if there is truth in a contemporary book, it doesn't sound the same depths. The classic is the standard. It's the past judging the present. Is it also the past with a strangle-hold on the present? You can argue that classic literature is our heritage: the best that's been thought and uttered; it tells us where we've been and puts us on the trail of our ancestors. But whose ancestors? Yours? I'm not so sure about mine.

There's a strong argument to be made that the classics have obscured the past, ignored or covered up the stories and histories of many people. It's been an Anglo-Saxon literature. The classics purport to tell us how we once lived and thought and felt, but they only tell us how some few of us once lived and felt.

Yet the classics go on being the classics. It says so here in the catalogue. If you believe in the classics, they are a secure and safe place to be. What a relief to see it clearly marked and labeled. No surprise packages. No burden of having to sort through all these new books with their rude, disquieting titles and distasteful, garish covers. How can you go wrong with a classic? Choose a classic and you're safe. No need to make choices. The classics are always appropriate. If you don't much get it, if your students don't get it at all, the fault is not with the classic but with the reader. Of course the Emperor is royally clad. But when was the last time you really looked?

All my life I've been burdened by an awareness of the Great Books of the Western World, the classics, priceless stuff, a mile long shelf of books it was my duty to read. I pitched in. I started early. But was it early enough? Wasn't it Thomas Hobbes's father who read to him when he was an infant? Or was it the guy who was so anti the French Revolution, Burnes, was it? Or was it William Blake? No, he was the poet. Edmund Burke, is that the guy? There are always parents like that around who get up earlier in the morning than anybody else and who start whispering lines from Shakespeare into their sleeping infant's ear.

Maybe that was my trouble from the start. My father never read to me. Add that to my list of grievances, Dad. My father never sat with me as I slept (what a sweet thought). He never whispered the grand old majestic lines to me. "And the rain was upon the earth forty days and forty nights." Maybe, right there, was where my trouble started. All my life I've been chasing the classics, and not making much progress. It's the classic nightmare: you're running as hard as you can, but your feet are stuck in mud. Every summer I tell myself I'm going to read Proust's *Remembrance of Things Past*, Joyce's *Ulysses*, maybe start on the complete works of Balzac. Every fall I think about taking a night course in English Lit: start at the beginning with the Greeks, do the myths, and work my way up. Homer to Freud.

I've tried. I've tried awfully hard. But maybe not hard enough. I'm left with a sense of guilt, a feeling that somehow I've failed. I've known the names a long time, since I was ten years old: Homer, Plato, Aristotle, Herodotus, Chaucer, Shakespeare. I warmed up with *Lamb's Tales from Shakespeare*. The first book I bought was a verse edition of *The Iliad*, with a wonderful illustration of a naked goddess on the frontispiece. I used to run around with a two-pound copy of Gibbon's *The Decline and Fall of the Roman Empire* under my arm, sometimes replaced by equally weighty copies of *Das Kapital* or Schopenhauer's *Studies in Pessimism*. If they didn't weigh at least two pounds, I wouldn't carry them. I had the misguided idea that girls were impressed by boys who carried big books. Sometimes I'd flip through the pages and read a little here and there or check out the table of contents, looking for anything that suggested sex or gore.

Young as I was, I already knew that to be conversant with the classics, even just knowing names, was to have a leg up on my fellows. If nothing else, I impressed myself with the books I was hauling around. I thought I was a hot ball of fire. Bennett Cerf's Modern Library Editions were my prize possessions. I owned Machiavelli's *The Prince* (that was a small one), but also *The Collected Works of Keats and Shelley*—or was it Shelley and Byron?

I dipped into these books. A spoonful. It was like putting a toe into the ocean. I got it, but what did I get? If it was a story, I paid attention, but, mostly, my eye wandered. I lacked whatever it took to master the classics. All my efforts convinced me that I was inadequate: too young, too stupid, too ill-prepared.

Fortunately I loved to read too much to be turned aside. I loved libraries; I loved books; I read everything I could put my hands on. But you've heard that story before: how the writer is brought to writing by his love of the printed word. What about kids whose connection to reading is still tentative and who, for whatever reason, don't love to read? The classics for them are maybe what grammar was to me. Befuddlement, pain, and confusion. I could never figure out what the teacher was talking about. "Nouns are used mainly as subjects of verbs, objects of verbs or prepositions, as compliments following a linking verb, as appositives, or as modifiers of other words." Grammar convinced me that I couldn't write, that it was useless to even try. How could I even think of writing when I couldn't keep adjectives, adverbs, and adverbial phrases straight?

I was a reader, but a writer? Me a writer? It was the wildest fantasy. I never voiced the thought, hardly let myself think it. I kept the dream of being a writer hidden, that poor, pale little voice locked away in a back bedroom of my mind. (Ouch. I sound like a country western singer. *In the back bedrooms of my mind . . .*)

As a boy I had a volume of Sophocles under my arm, but I was reading the Modern Library edition of Eugene O'Neill's plays. While floundering through Chaucer's sweet lines (my five fingers stuck in the glossary), I was also reading Damon Runyon, de Maupassant, and Erskine Caldwell. Caldwell was great. He had sex.

I read a little here, a little there. A smattering of this and that. Was I educated? There was so much I still didn't know . . . and what I knew wouldn't do. I was convinced that anything that mattered—no, *everything* that mattered—was in these books. The classics would teach me how to think, how to write, even how to be with girls.

If I didn't understand the classics, the fault was with me. I read books on how to read the Great Books. I read Adler's *How to Read a Book*. I didn't trust my own reactions or opinions. The classics, after all, were the classics. They were perfection. What did I know? I kept reading. For a while it was the Russians: Turgenev, Gogol, Dostoyevsky, Tolstoy. I read *Crime and Punishment* from start to finish. Next, *The Brothers Karamazov*, then *Anna Karenina*. I was twelve years old. I discovered I had a talent for reading and thinking about something else. I loved *Crime and Punishment*, but I skated blissfully through the long philosophical debates. Sometimes I'd find that I'd read several pages and couldn't remember a word. Maybe I was taking it all in subliminally, like baby Hobbes in the crib.

In school there were more classics. Longfellow's *Evangeline*, read aloud by an enraptured teacher. *Great Expectations* and *A Tale of Two Cities*. In sophomore English, it was *Julius Caesar* and in my junior year *Hamlet* and *Macbeth*.

Between the classics and grammar I could barely put a sentence together without being frozen with fear. Words mattered, but they were like bullets. They could destroy me. Each one had to be perfectly aimed and placed exactly on target. I would hold the words in my head and consider this one and then that one, reject them both, then come up with another word. In those days I wrote very short pieces.

It took me years to take myself seriously as a writer. My standards were so exalted anything I wrote had to be puny, worthless in comparison. The moment I sat at the typewriter, the Seventy-Six Greatest Authors were there, standing above me, all male, all white-bearded, all wearing long white togas and holding their two-pound tomes over my head. I worked so hard to write anything and it was so futile. I was trying to manipulate words. It was the very antithesis of what writing should be. I treated words like objects, rolling them into place like stones—and it was all uphill. Remember Sisyphus? (How's that for a classical allusion?)

To write well is to catch an image, a movement, a flow. Written language is an attempt to give form to and make visible what is liquid, unending, formless. To become a writer, I needed to be loose, to free a flow of imagery and rhythm. I needed to make mistakes, to allow myself the freedom to write poorly. But how could I even think this? There was no poor writing in the classics.

There was no process, no learning, no failure, no stumbling, no hesitation, no doubts.

The classics, I believed, were written in stone, perfect on the first take. God didn't rewrite the Ten Commandments. There was no draft, no revision, no editing. That was the way I regarded the classics—Great Writing that poured out in a single perfect inspired moment. The Moonlight Sonata as interpreted by Hollywood. I only became a writer when I finally said to myself: Damn the classics, damn the great writers, damn the delusion that what you write has to be perfect. No judging, no comparing, just get the words out the best way you can. But even then I still couldn't simply say I was writing. I had to be a pompous ass and say I was writing *The Great American Novel*.

I learned how to write when I accepted that the first writing, a draft, was only that—a beginning, a reaching, an approximation of what I wanted. Writing, I had to learn, was a process. There was always another chance, as many as I had energy and inventiveness and patience for. I learned that there is no right word. Words are endless. They come and come. They're like the wind, the air we breath. We breathe and the words come out. They can be gathered and arranged in so many ways. Revising a line is like dropping a stone into a pool. One ripple leads to another and another. There's no end to the process.

I had to learn to accept my own words. It wasn't a matter of being a major or minor anything. I was writing. I was telling stories. I was doing what writers do. Writers write, just as singers sing and a man with a shovel digs.

When I first caught a glimmer of these thoughts, when I finally set myself free, I was at a typewriter, a Smith-Corona manual I had used in college. I don't know if it was morning or night, but there was a blank sheet of paper in place, waiting for that flow to begin, that flood of language that I hoped was in me.

I sat there. After a while I wrote, "Isabel, you'll never know what you did to me. How could you, I never spoke to you."

Isabel was a girl in my sixth-grade class in PS 96 in the Bronx. That year I followed her everywhere, but never spoke to her.

"Isabel, you'll never know." I loved that line. Here I was in my thirties, married and a father of three children, talking in the voice of my twelve-year-old self. I was here and I was there. I was in the present and I was reliving the past.

What is literature but the marking and reflection of our lives? It's paying attention, framing, distillation, and celebration. Literature is about the world we inhabit. In literature, we hear the voices and spirit of our times. We need to hear those voices. The young, who still know so little and want so much, hunger for them. Literature is an ordering of the tumble-jumble of our thoughts, our fantasies and fears, our ecstasies and exaltations. It offers answers to the big questions and the trifling ones as well.

The classics, the great literary works of the past, are too limiting for our needs. The classics don't belong in the junior high curriculum. Literature should be at the heart of an English curriculum, but that literature should be contemporary. The classics are too distant from the lives of kids. They need to be interpreted, and their difficulty becomes something to be feared. But, mainly, the classics give the wrong message to students. Too many kids emerge from their contact with the classics feeling that literature is something forbidden, difficult, and without relevance to their lives. They think it belongs to an elite, and they reject it, reject all literature. That's a loss we can't afford.

Schools underscore this alienation when they make the classics part of the A Track, funnel them to the college bound, the elite students. The others, it's hoped, will at least graduate able to read and write.

Everyone loses. The A Trackers lose because they believe they really are an elite. And the other kids learn that literature and high culture are weapons that can be used against them. The Arts have always been a way of supporting hierarchies. But what a misuse of art and literature. Literature belongs to all of us. It's a scandal if a student graduates having no use for books or literature, and hating to read.

Let me say it again. Literature belongs to all of us. To the kids and to their parents. Not only the enjoyment of it, but the creation of it as well. Real people make literature. Do I dare say it? They even make money doing it.

There's a connection between literature and commerce. This is something the classicists don't like to talk about. Writers write for money, and book publishers hope to make a profit. This was ever so. Shakespeare wrote his plays for a paying public. Dickens wrote his novels for newspaper serialization. And Balzac, who was always in debt, worked through the night, keeping himself awake with strong cups of coffee. Books aren't produced in Heaven. Writers think about their audience, and they think about their market. But for the people who revere Great Books and set them on a pedestal, there's always a taint, a sniff of common dirt, when money and books are joined.

Literature is greater, broader, wider, more encompassing than the classics. Literature is an ocean. The classics are like an inland sea. We don't need "great" books to bring our kids to literature. We need readable books that enchant and inform and move kids to want more.

Why teach the classics? Why struggle to make meaningful what belongs in a history program or in an advanced literature class? At a time when our kids are not reading, when we need all our inventiveness, imagination, and flexibility to keep the desire to read alive, the classics keep us doing things in old, tired ways.

Much has been heard from the few, little from the many of humankind. Literature needs these other voices. Blacks, women, Native Americans, Hispanics, and the voices of children and teenagers. It's only in contemporary literature, in books that are being written now and will be written in the future, that we have a chance of hearing these voices—these voices who are us.

Every reader's response matters.

Photo by Jim Mayfield

2

Ride the Horse in the Direction It's Going

Sandy Asher

TEENAGERS have to figure out who they are and where and how they fit into the world. That's their job. It's hard work. It makes them feel raw and vulnerable, and a lot of what they're finding out about themselves and life in general isn't all they'd hoped it would be, so they're often grumpy. But that's what the rest of us have to work with, as parents, writers, teachers, and friends.

"Ride the horse," we're told, "in the direction it's going." In teaching young adults, it seems to me, that bit of folk wisdom translates as "make the most of the quest for self, and tred cautiously around the ego."

That comes easily enough when our youngsters are babies exploring their fingers and toes. We're all approval and encouragement then. But when they start searching for their own hearts and minds, we get nervous. We call them selfish and self-centered, and we're right. But so are they. Our discomfort with their single-mindedness won't change it; self-discovery is the direction in which they have got to go.

Common sense suggests we go with them, and yet, the exact opposite is all too often standard procedure in literature classrooms. All manner of distractions, programmed into the system to get

11

everyone through the syllabus and the tests, discourage young people from finding themselves in what they read and, at the same time, make them feel inadequate as readers—when they already feel inadequate in just about every other way they can think of.

Some time ago, I was interviewed for an article in *The Journal of Reading*. The interviewer asked me how I felt about having my books taught in classrooms. I had to admit I have mixed feelings about being "required reading." I can't deny feeling flattered when a teacher finds something I've written worthy of presenting to his or her class. Without a doubt, I'm pleased to have new readers introduced to my books.

But I worry about the unpleasant connotations of "required reading." Suddenly, the reader and I are no longer alone; there are outside forces affecting our time together, changing the reader's experience of the book, affecting—for better or worse—our efforts to reach one another.

I worry, for instance, about the medicinal factor: Take this, it's good for you. Young people don't like taking medicine. The mind and heart, like the mouth, automatically clamp shut. It helps when whoever's doing the prescribing knows just how much sugar it takes to open them—*a lot*!

I worry about the search for spare parts: Like cars raised on racks at a service station, stories are disassembled and reduced to their various components, handy for testing or carting away for other lessons, but no longer equal to the whole. An example that still gives me the willies: A while back, I was invited to read one of my short stories to a class. They were a wonderful audience, responding with laughter and applause, just as I'd hoped they would. And then their teacher broke in with, "Boys and girls, did you notice how Mrs. Asher made use of her *adjectives?*"

The light in those eager young eyes died. They nodded dutifully, because they were "good" students, and they knew the one and only correct answer to her question was "yes." But they hadn't noticed any adjectives. They'd been too busy bringing their individual, wholehearted responses to my story, and she'd invalidated those responses, squashed them flat with her rummaging-for-spare-parts approach.

Next time you're caught up in a wonderful book, try noticing the adjectives. Or the punctuation. Or even the similes and metaphors. It's *distracting*. It breaks the connection between reader and story. If reading is addictive, that might well be the cure, but a cure is not what we're after here! The words are there to tell the story; the story isn't there to display an assortment of words. And yet, that's often the way literature is "taught."

Teachers have to teach grammar, punctuation, and spelling in some sort of context, of course, and I admit there were days when one of my teachers pointed out a metaphor or symbol and shed glorious light on the books we were reading. But there's a difference between illuminating stories through heightened comprehension and plucking out details haphazardly. All the technique in the world is useless if the reader isn't moved by the characters and their story.

I worry, also, about bibliotherapy, a combination of the medicinal factor and the search for spare parts. Bibliotherapy (or "Take Two Books and Call Me in the Morning") capitalizes on the human need to categorize: animal, vegetable, mineral, vertebrate, invertebrate, our team, their team, all of the above, none of the above. Categorization is a necessary tool for organizing the vast amount of material we must process in the course of a lifetime. But can one honestly say of a novel, this book is about death, this book is about learning disabilities, this book is about child abuse? Would we suggest, adult to adult, that Tolstoy's *War and Peace* is a book about war? Or a book about peace? Or even a book about war *and* peace? I think not. What good adult literature is about is its unforgettable characters, the richness of their lives, the value and meaning of their existence. Should a book become less than that when its reader is a young adult?

Unfortunately, both young adults and the books they read (particularly young adult novels) are often classified by problem. Parent, teacher, and librarian, willing or not, are cast as therapists and encouraged to match subject matter to child: divorce to divorce, abuse to abuse, handicap to handicap. It's a well-intended effort to help young people in trouble, but I fear it's misguided.

I don't know about you, but when I'm depressed, a depressing book is the last thing I want to read. Coming from the bedside of a dying friend or relative, for instance, I do not want to curl up with a book about a dying friend or relative. And if by some chance I do find myself in the company of such a book, I'm as likely to be disturbed by it as comforted. It may miss the mark and fail to do justice to my pain, or it may come unbearably close to an open wound.

Maybe I'm unusual in this. Maybe young people are more open to facing hard facts at difficult moments. But I suspect not. One's timing, therefore, would have to be exquisite to match up book, reader, and therapeutic instant.

Sometimes the right book at the right time from the right person helps. Sure. But bibliotherapy as a systematic way of viewing books and young people is what troubles me. It diminishes both book and reader. Neither human beings nor books should be categorized by single issues. There is far more to each, and that complexity must be respected.

A lifetime reading habit, on the other hand, *can* build broad survival skills, and this is particularly true in the teen years. Novels provide ways of interpreting life and living it. Almost all young adult novels, for instance, leave both reader and main character with feelings of hope. Determination and effort, understanding, and a healthy sense of humor generally move YA main characters out of danger and within reach of their goals. That's a life-affirming attitude that becomes part of young readers exposed to it. But the process takes time, and the growth happens internally, as readers pick and choose what they need from books, consciously and unconsciously. It's not something that can be applied externally, like first aid.

The system that doses young readers with medicine and therapy and requires the breaking down of novels into utilitarian parts also sets up teachers as Sole Living Authorities, expected to dish out the One True Vision of a book and then test for it.

I don't think many teachers are actually comfortable in this role, although they may not know how to avoid it, but I have met a few who played it to the hilt. To this day, my own confidence as a reader suffers from having been made to feel like a fool because I didn't see what they saw in the books, plays, and poems we studied.

There they stood in front of class after class, books clutched to their bosoms (as if to say, "Mine! Mine!"), calling on me when I did not have my hand raised, probing for, insisting on, the one and only right answers to questions they'd posed—answers they already knew and wouldn't tell the class until we'd been sufficiently humbled, convinced that because we could not read their minds, we could not read.

I remember being taught poetry that way and learning to hate it. What, a teacher demanded of my high school English class, did the word *snow* mean in A. E. Housman's line "to see the cherry hung with snow?"

Pity us. We thought *snow* meant *snow*. Fifty-five minutes and a barrage of confusing questions later ("What color are cherry blossoms?" "Could it mean the blossoms themselves?" "What time of year do cherry blossoms blossom?"), delivered with what could have been a smile but what looked to me, in my utter frustration, like an all-knowing smirk, the word *snow* didn't mean anything anymore. The entire poem was hung with lead.

Looking back, I assume she thought she was teaching us that words in poetry can have many meanings. What she taught us instead was to read poetry one word at a time, painfully aware at each and every turn that we were probably misinterpreting it, and never mind responding to the whole poem as a whole person. I decided the entire point of poetry was to trick students. Somehow, poets were in cahoots with teachers, providing them with insights they denied everyone else. Next time you see a poem, I warned myself, run for your life. If it hits you, it will leave you feeling stupid.

I'd hate to see Michael Paeglis or any of my other characters used as an invitation to a game students can't win. I'd like them to care about what happens to him. I hope they'll experience and understand their own lives in new ways for having experienced and understood his. I'd like them to feel free to interpret *Everything Is Not Enough* and my other books according to their own insights; whatever they find worth relating to is okay with me.

And it's perfectly valid for them not to like Michael and his book at all. It seems to me that presenting a thoughtful argument against a book or play or poem is just as valuable a learning experience for the reader as regurgitating the official line in favor of it. Even if it's something by Shakespeare. Even if it's something by me.

I have always maintained that my books are only half finished when written, that the other half is in the reading, what each reader brings to the story out of his or her own experience. I offer as proof of my theory my son's preschool rendition of the Pledge of Allegiance: "I pledge allegiance to the flag of the United States of America, and to the republic for which it stands, one nation, under the haystack, fast asleep."

To a preschooler, that makes about as much sense as anything else he's called upon to say or do in the course of a day to make adults happy. What is a preschooler's allegiance worth to the re-public anyway?

To a first- or second-grader, "one nation, under the haystack" might be disconcerting: "Is that right? It could be right. Did I say it wrong?"

To a third- or fourth-grader, it would be hysterically funny, the laughter heightened by relief at not being that little and that dumb anymore.

To a fifteen-year-old, feeling a bit parental as a babysitter, the mistake might be kind of sweet.

And to a farm-rights activist, it could be a political slogan worthy of a banner: "One Nation, Under the Haystack, *Fast Asleep.*"

The words remain the same; the interpretations make a con-siderable difference. Writers try very hard to control that second half of their books, to maintain a clarity that encourages certain interpretations, of course, but the intensity of their effort only confirms that the second half—the reader's half—exists.

Every reader's response *matters*. Writers *need* readers to complete the work of the book. That's not something we're often taught in school. In the classroom, we're expected to revere great writers, to approach them with feelings of awe. But we don't spend much time noticing that without readers, lots of readers, all kinds of readers, their work would remain incomplete.

A young reader who knows that feels powerful in his or her reading, and *should*. That feeling of power feeds perfectly into the teenager's need to establish an identity, a sense of self and self-worth. The way each student responds helps to define the book, but it also helps to define the student. Get to know a book; get to know yourself. Who could resist an offer like that, especially in the fail-safe environment of a classroom where individual responses are valued?

Putting the young reader at the center of the reading experience benefits everyone. The writer gets a fair shake at reaching that reader—without distractions, extractions, and the bitter taste of medicine coming between them. Teachers are relieved of the need to know everything, all the time, or deliver the same lesson, hour after hour, or even choose every book that's read. Discussion ques-tions can move in all directions around the room, eliciting refreshing new answers from every reader, including the teacher: Which character are you most likely to remember and why? How would you have handled the character's problems with his or her parents, teachers, or friends? How are you different from that character? Have you had similar experiences? In short, *you* choose what this story has to say to *you*.

People tend to repeat activities they enjoy—even when they're teenagers and the activity is reading. Relaxed, everyone-into-the-pool conversation about books is fun. Searching for a single, hidden right answer is not. Learning that your own personal reaction to a story, play, or poem matters is fun. Having the focus predetermined for you is not. Watching movies of a story is fun. Acting out a story can be fun. Book talks presented with honest excitement and laced with intriguing sample passages are fun.

Fun is a good thing. Young people learn through play—at eight months, at eight years, and at eighteen. *Ride the horse in the direction it's going.* We need to use their natural tendency to play to get them where we—and they—want them to go. Lighten up, and we can all enjoy the trip!

The teachers who made me care about literature showed me their own delight. They embarked on journeys of discovery and invited the class to do the same. Their faces glowed; they made the trip seem too good to miss. They wore their hearts on their sleeves. They were crestfallen when the class didn't laugh at Chaucer's bawdiness or weep for Romeo and Juliet. But that was okay. They were adults; they could allow us our opinions, knowing full well that what we thought at age sixteen would change by age twenty and change again later, as our perceptions broadened and deepened.

Meanwhile, they got a kick out of letting us wrestle with their truths and our own, and occasionally we were even able to convince them to reconsider. Our lack of sophistication didn't dismay them, and sometimes they saw it as an advantage. The less they insisted on being Sole Living Authorities, the more willing we were to acknowledge how much they did know. They admitted that no two of us would ever end up at quite the same place in our literary journeys. We couldn't; we were different travelers. But we were all readers together.

So much of what we call education has to do with stuffing information into young heads and then checking on it periodically to see whether it's stayed put or fallen out. But what about what's already in there—observations, interpretations, imagination, vision, emotion? There aren't too many standardized tests for all of that. And yet great advances in every field are made by individuals who know their facts but who also have access to and confidence in their own unique responses to those facts. Unfettered reading is one way to practice that ability to respond, one way to explore outer and inner universes at the same time.

Am I suggesting that there be no more required reading? No, I'm not. I'm glad those teachers who loved certain authors and works shared them with me. I appreciate having my own books introduced to new readers. Enthusiasm isn't threatening; it's attractive. I do think young adults should be given more opportunities to choose what they read and to respond to it as individuals, even to dislike it. Respect isn't threatening, either, and it can move both ways across an open book.

Teachers must teach their courses; adolescents must establish their identities. Rejection is a distinct possibility, for everyone involved. So is excitement about reading. It's a gamble. To "ride the horse in the direction it's going"—toward self-discovery and with a healthy sense of fun—strikes me as the surest bet.

Photo by Ruth Putter

We Americans love ice cream. And the way we love ice cream is the way we should love reading. Passionate involvement, willingness to try all flavors, a lighting of the eyes, eating it in all seasons, a pint always in the freezer.

3

The Ice-Cream Syndrome (aka Promoting Good Reading Habits)

Norma Fox Mazer

WHEN I write, the faster I can hook the reader, the better. I want to hook the reader like a fish, swiftly and firmly. But wait. Is that what I really want? I remember too well the day I gave up fishing: the small bass flopping in my hand as I worked to pull out the hook caught in its mouth, my youngest daughter's sickened grimace, and my own sudden awareness of this sport as another bloody business.

No, that is not a good metaphor for reading. Let me begin again. With water and fish, but differently.

When I write, I want to entice the reader into another world. I want my readers to fall into what I've written like falling into water, to go down and down and down, to enter that underwater universe, to be transformed, to breathe like a sea creature, effortlessly slipping and sliding and swimming, a fish among fish.

I remember that watery world; I remember myself curled in the chair in the living room after supper with my book: lost, gone, transported, so far away that my mother's voice calling me to dry the dishes was nothing but a faint burr, a buzz like that of a fly on a hot summer day.

"I've called you six times already," she would say.

Had she? It came as a surprise to me. I was supposed to dry the dishes and act cheerful about it. It was a hated task. Still, I wasn't ignoring my mother. I just didn't hear her. I was somewhere else. But now that I *was* back in the real world, I had to go to the bathroom urgently.

A ploy, my mother thought, but I wasn't up to that kind of deception. It was simply a Law of Nature that drying dishes and a full bladder invariably coincided. In the bathroom, I would stare at the witch in the doorknob, scared and fascinated, hoping she wouldn't come out. I'd get lost in thinking about her. It was almost as good as reading.

Soon, another call from the universe of dishes and mothers. "Norma! Are you going to stay in there forever?" Had it been a real question, a choice, I would have answered YES! Daydreaming and reading were joy, they were reward and temptation, and every night, especially, they were *not* drying hateful silverware, which sullenly turned rusty if left undried.

Let me get back on track. I didn't agree to do an essay on what reading meant to me as a child, but on "Promoting Good Reading Habits." *Promoting Good Reading Habits?* Sounds so stuffy. Makes me want to barf. Oh, how *childish*. Well, yes, but isn't that the point?

A so-called "good" reading "habit" is something which, like how to roller skate and how to lick an ice-cream cone (from the bottom up, slowly turning the cone counterclockwise), we ought to learn in childhood. That's when we learn things from the heart, with zest, energy, eagerness, openness, and joy, with the stamina and unself-conscious grace of the child.

Good Reading Habits—from now on to be known as GRH— begin in the home. Parents need to read to their children when they're still going "goo goo gah gah." The first book Harry and I bought for our first baby was *Mother Goose*. Long before she was putting words into sentences, our baby girl knew all those rhymes, and when I sat down with her, she would riffle the pages impatiently to find the rhymes she particularly liked. I remember waking early in the morning and hearing her babble in secret baby language, with here and there a nursery rhyme word clearly thrown in. By the time she was a year and a half old, I'd hear her telling herself stories. And when she was four, she taught herself to read.

Okay, she's a writer now; words and rhymes and stories are in her blood. You can certainly make a case for that, but it's also true that her two sisters and her brother learned to read and love reading the same way. We read to them from the time they were tiny, whatever books we had at home, whatever we found in the library that was fun to read to babies and little kids. (I think we broke all of them in on those same Mother Goose rhymes.)

I remember one small daughter sobbing brokenheartedly over the story of a little dog with a bandage over its eyes. Every night she asked to have this story read to her. "But, honey, it makes you cry," I'd say. "I won't cry," she'd declare stoutly. "I just want to hear it." So we'd read this book, and the moment the dog got the bandage over its eyes, she broke into tears of grief. I remember walking with another daughter and reciting Robert Louis Stevenson's poems with her. "I have a little shadow that goes in and out with me . . ." Why these poems? Because *I* liked them.

There were always books in our house, as there had always been books in my growing-up home. When I was a girl, every night everyone in my family sat or lay somewhere—in their favorite chair or on the floor or in their bed—and they read. There was never any question that all three of us Fox girls were to be readers like our parents. We were, and we are, to this day. From this experience, with no statistics or studies to back it up, I long ago concluded that a love of reading (and along with it GRH) starts in the home with the parents' reading for themselves, to themselves, to each other, and to their children.

So what has that to do with the beleaguered teacher faced with a class of thirty or thirty-five students (and faced not once, not twice, but four or five times a day), in which maybe a handful of those thirty-five kids come from homes where reading is preferred to TV, where there are books in residence, and where people talk about books and look on them as a source of pleasure?

Is the teacher supposed to throw up her or his hands because in the Real World, the world of teenagers and video, teenagers and TV, teenagers and Nintendo, teenagers and movies, they didn't learn GRH at home? And why didn't they? Why do so many teens regard nearly everything as amusing, entertaining, juicy, and pleasurable, except books? Is it simply because anything they *don't* do in school is terrifically desirable? Or is it because they live in a different world than the one in which we adults grew up?

Remember Abraham Lincoln studying his books by firelight? Though my generation grew up far from the log-cabin world, in some ways our world was closer to Lincoln's than to the world of kids today. We lived in a world in which our knowledge and perceptions came to us largely through the printed word, while kids today live in a world in which a vast amount of their perceptions and knowledge come to them visually. TV has made that difference. It has changed the face of the world and kids, as well.

I have a feeling that there's something genetically encoded in human beings that makes moving objects utterly compelling. I've seen people sitting in their lawn chairs, watching the traffic on the highway. Our ancestors watched the herds of moving animals, alert for food and danger, and though the food comes to us packaged now and the danger is no longer over the horizon but in the air and water, we are still and always drawn to watching.

Kids, teenagers, parents—Americans in general—watch TV on an average of something like six hours a day. Where do they find the time, with everything else they do? And why? Because TV is accessible and demands little of us. Press a button and the images spring to "life." A poor substitute for the real thing, but who remembers, once under the spell of the visual? Add to that the allure of voices and music, which also come so comfortingly over the tube, and TV becomes nearly irresistible. Sit down, lie down, put yourself at ease, let the eyes take it all in, and here's the "world" coming to you effortlessly.

Reading is just not that easy. Reading takes a tiny bit of effort. There is no remote-control reading. No buttons to press. We have to pick up the book, open it, look at the words, let the distractions around us fade, willingly enter the world the author presents, fall into the story, imagine and accept the characters, allow them to quicken in the brain. All this is active, not passive.

Teachers and librarians have figured all this out already. And they have a grab-bag of techniques and ideas to entice kids into reading. One of the things a lot of teachers are doing now is encouraging their students to write letters to authors. As a result, I receive far more mail from people I don't know than from my friends and family. The letters from kids are sometimes funny, sometimes prim, sometimes really sad ("I'm fourteen and my mother kicked me out of the house . . ."), and other times immensely satisfying

("I never read a book all the way through before your book, but now I will read again.").

And every once in a while, they're impossible to categorize, like the one I received from a boy named Donny. In a pinched hand, he wrote, "I read your book. It was good. I have some questions. Why did her sister get pregnant? Who won the jackpot? That part confused me. Did her father have to do drugs? Please write back."

Donny's whole letter confused *me*, since there were no pregnant sisters, no jackpots, and no father who did drugs in the book he mentioned. Donny had either decided that all young adult books were one young adult book, or he knew how to get around a teacher who hadn't read the book either. In either case, one thing was clear about him. He did not have GRH.

Before I go any further, I have to change the intended title of this essay: "Promoting Good Reading Habits." Three out of those four words are giving me trouble. *Reading* is not one of them.

Let me start with *promoting*. This word brings to mind excessive commercialism and advertising, things I think have gotten out of hand in our society. It makes reading sound like something we writers and teachers are going to make megabucks on, or something we want to put over on teenagers, the way the beer people put drinking over on them, making it appear cozy and friendly and harmless with their little bulldogs and cute bouncy ads.

As for *habits*, that word somehow stops me dead every time. Habits are things we don't even know we have, but that are annoying to other people. I asked Harry to tell me a habit of mine. It didn't take him two seconds to answer. "Putting things away, putting everything in its damn place." He likes to let things "lay where they lie." His words. My words are "pile up, spill over, fall off." My words are also "junk heap," as in, "Your desk is a. . . ." He claims he can find exactly what he wants any time he wants it. So why is he always crying, "Where are my glasses?" He only has five pairs scattered in strategic places around the house. (Excuse this diversion. I know a dignified essay is no place for marital bickering.)

Even when people talk about "good" habits, it's always something we do because we've been warned of the otherwise unpleasant results. If we knew we could ignore our teeth and they'd still stay white, shining, and healthy, how many of us would bother brushing? Habits seem to be something we either can't control or make ourselves do because the consequences of *not* doing are so distasteful. So who wants a reading *habit*? A reading lust would be more my idea.

Now about the word *good*, admittedly a serviceable word, without which we'd all be in trouble. (Try counting the number of times you use it in just a single day.) The problem with *good* is that good is, well, good. We're brought up and we bring our kids up to be good: meaning truthful, obedient, nice, kind, generous, considerate, moral, trustworthy, etc., etc. Who can argue with that? Not me. But to the restless, energetic, brash, confused young who are trying so desperately to make themselves individuals, to burst out of the powerless prison of their childhood into the longed for "freedom" of adulthood, *good* sounds, face it, blaaaah! Boring! Pallid! Dull!

I said I'd change the title of this essay. I was sitting here, considering "Love of Reading," when the words "The Ice-Cream Syndrome" popped into my mind. I didn't know what they meant, but I liked them. As in a lot of my writing, they came as a gift. My part was to figure out what this gift meant.

I started thinking about last week when I stopped in at my favorite health-food store. At the check-out counter was the very tall, very lean and bony, raw-faced young man, the one with the silky sixties ponytail and the Greenpeace T-shirt. Suddenly, between ringing up the whole-wheat English muffins (for Harry) and the raw almonds (for me), he stopped punching the register and turned to me with a look of pure ecstasy. He's younger by several years than my youngest daughter, but the expression on his face, his eyes lit with passion, told me that he was about to deliver an ardent declaration of love.

I blinked, thinking of the four pounds I'd recently lost by getting back my racquetball game. Did it make that much difference? Or was it my white T-shirt that said (mysteriously; I bought it at a thrift shop) BROOKS? Or was it the youthful, merry way I'd rolled up my pants legs? Looking into his ecstatic gaze, I prepared to tell him (gently, of course) that I was flattered, but gee, gosh, I not only had a longtime husband, but four kids and two grandkids, and well, you know . . .

He broke into speech. "Häagen-Dazs Honey Vanilla," he said

in hushed tones. *"No sugar.* I ate a pint last night. It's . . ." He couldn't go on. Ecstasy overcame him; he was speechless at the thought of such perfection—ice cream with *no sugar*—and simply shook his head in awed wonder. "You want some?" he asked, shining at me.

Well, no, I was just then off for a three-hour drive on a blistering day, but that's not the point of the story. The point is that we Americans love ice cream. And the way we love ice cream is the way we should love reading. Passionate involvement, willingness to try all flavors, a lighting of the eyes, eating it in all seasons, a pint always in the freezer. Kids learn to love ice cream when they're still in diapers and strollers, and the giant person whose duty it is to make them happy leans down one hot day and says, "Take a lick, sweetie pie."

I remember the magic of learning to read; I remember the moment it happened to me, not in public school, but in Sunday School. (How odd that it happened there to me, who rarely enters a temple, who calls herself an agnostic.) I was about four years old, sitting in a tiny green chair, listening to the teacher reading and looking down at my book, at the picture of poor Joseph lying in the ditch in his pretty coat. And the black squiggles became words. At four, then, I experienced one of the supreme moments of my life. I, a small person in a huge world, had found something I would never let go of.

Perhaps I am a writer today because reading and stories en-thralled me at such an early age. Did it arouse in me the desire to similarly enthrall others? I have never known why, at the age of thirteen, I became irresistibly drawn to writing, why it was then that the desire to become "a writer" (whatever that was, whatever that meant: I had no idea) crystallized in me. Now I look back and understand that reading was control, writing was control. In a world in which I felt little control, in which I was often baffled, hurt, confused, inhibited, afraid, desperate, words were powerful. I used them, played with them, learned them, savored them.

What *are* good reading habits? Now that I've got my fancy ice-cream title, let me hop back to "Promoting Good Reading Habits" and take another look at it. Yes, I want kids to have GRH. Kids are my audience. I write for them. I need them. Where would I be without them? Writers never have enough readers, and never never enough with GRH!

So what does GRH mean? Reading with joy, anticipation, eagerness; it means picking up a book because it looks interesting not because it's thin; it means feeling naked without a book in your hip pocket or your purse; and it means realizing that you are never, ever, bored if you're a reader.

How to promote good reading habits? Doesn't the whole thing boil down to one sentence? *If a kid loves reading, that kid will have good reading habits.* A equals B. If you love reading, you read. So teach them to love reading, make them love it and—wait, whoa, halt! I take that back. Delete *teach*, delete *make*. I was careless to write that. Those words, the ideas they embody, are the antithesis of what I believe. Love of reading is not something we can force on anyone. We can't "teach" love of reading. Nor what "should" be read.

I said my own children all loved reading. They did, but their choice of reading was sometimes problematic. My son read comic books almost exclusively the year he was ten. His comic book collection, stacked as high as his nose in his closet, put me in despair. How could Harry and I have a kid whose tastes were so, well, *low*?

Once I stood in his room staring at those comics and thinking of a bonfire. What a thought for someone who abhors censorship and remembers with particular horror reading about the burning of "bad" books in Nazi Germany! "Bad" books had meant books by Jews, "liberals," books by anyone who didn't uphold Aryan "supremacy." I didn't have a bonfire, of course, and, in time, without any help from me, my son began reading other things: baseball books, *The Harvard Lampoon*, *Trout Fishing in America*, *The Bghavada Gita*, *That Was Then, This is Now*. Really, I don't remember what he read. I never paid much attention to what my kids read because I had a basic attitude: Oh, you're reading. Great, so am I.

Now my son, grown, reads rather widely. He loves reading, he loves stories, and I rarely go wrong with one of his recommendations for a book. Half our phone conversations are about books. He's introduced us to the best mystery writers. Lately, he read *War and Peace*, a novel that has always daunted me by its sheer size (1400 closely printed pages). When I mentioned this to him, he said, "But, Mom, it's a good story." So I've taken the book up and discovered he's right. *It's a good story.* Yes! That's the foundation, isn't it? I'm not saying love of reading and GRH will bring all your teenagers to *War and Peace*. That's a matter of taste, choice, and the individual. I am saying there's no "teaching," there's no "promoting" reading without a good story.

Reading often has all kinds of moral qualities attached to it. It "widens your horizons." It "puts you in touch with our literary heritage." What else does reading do that's good for you? Oh, yes, it keeps your brain alert; it exercises your imagination, improves your vocabulary, not to speak of your reading scores on those damnable but necessary (we think) state tests. And more: it gets you in decent working order through this society of ours, which is structured on the assumption that the citizens are literate. As much of a stranglehold as TV has on our minds, the written word is still cheaper and remains a standby, a staple, a necessity for advertising, for charitable appeals, for news, for information, for getting a driver's license, renting an apartment, applying for health insurance, or understanding your bills.

Those are all good reasons to know how to read well. But something is left out. Love of reading. How do you get someone from this TV generation to read spontaneously? How do you get someone from this TV generation to read at all, without shoving a book into his hands and ordering him to read it? That's definitely a rotten way to go about promoting GRH.

You probably know that, but to drive home the point, think about food: we tend to like what we know, to be cautious with the unknown (chocolate-covered ants, grilled grasshoppers). When I go into the classroom and tell kids I ate a live ant in aid of my "research" for *Saturday the Twelfth of October*, they always let out a long, collective, disgusted groan. "Gross," they cry, rolling their eyes and making gagging sounds.

I ask them if they don't want to know what that ant tasted like, and then I tell them: crunchy and sour. More groaning and gagging. I'm sure they're all thinking with relief of fatty bad-for-you hamburgers and nice greasy worse-for-you chips. But suppose they were in a class in Cuisine, and it was mandatory to eat that ant? Do you think they'd want to go on to other exotic stuff after being forced to ingest a crunchy ant (alive, at that)?

I wouldn't. What is ordered, what is forced on us, what is required becomes anathema. We all want to make our own choices. But if, in your cuisines of the world class, you could, by some relaxed magic, inculcate in your kids a love of different foods, an excitement about trying out "strange" things, they might even go for the ant on their own. Or some of them might. Others might tend toward buffalo meat. Or goat cheese.

To govern one's own life, to direct it, to understand that you have made a choice and that the choice is there to be made, to empower yourself (to use a buzzword) is what growing up is all about. To give teenagers the knowledge that they can choose is to give them power and control over themselves, and there is nothing more important.

Let them choose their own books. Have a library of paperbacks in the classroom, on the windowsill or on your desk, or on a shelf along the wall. The books are there and they're available. And read them yourself. Recommending comes from the heart. Enthusiasm is contagious. Strong feelings, either for or against, are interesting. Ask for your students' help in reading the books. Take their opinions seriously. Involve them in the process of selecting books, of weighing and assessing, of thinking about who is likely to enjoy which book and why.

So . . . a library in your classroom—and it's varied; it's got all kinds of stories, a wide range, something for every taste. You're reading the books, and so are the students. And you're talking about the books, and you're reading out loud, too. Read to the class five minutes a day, maybe as soon as you take attendance. Read them something that has them hanging by their toes. Read them something funny or mysterious or sensational or weird or dramatic. Read them something that makes them want to know *and then what happened?*

They'll listen to you . . . or they won't. Of course your hope is to read something so compelling they can't help listening. But basic to the whole process is choice. They must choose to listen. They can also choose not to listen. They must choose what they read, and they must be free to discard what they don't like. Which certainly doesn't mean you hold back your opinions. You're there to talk, persuade, recommend, and, okay, even *promote* if it suits your style.

You're creating something by doing all this—an atmosphere, an aura, a place where books and reading are important. If you're reading and your kids are reading, and reading and books are being talked about, even the reluctant ones are going to read. Teenagers have to do what everyone else is doing.

What you're doing is in the way of being a guide. A connection. A link. You're linking up kids and books. When the right connection is made, when children find a book that gives them that thrill of seclusion and absorption, that wraps them in the words that create a story, a world apart, then they're going to want that thrill again. And this is the way they develop GRH.

The story . . . the story is all. This is why we watch TV and go to movies. This is why *People* magazine has become the one magazine we all share. *It tells stories.* This is why kids talk all the time, for the stories they tell and the stories they hear. This is why they sit in class with their mouths hanging open, staring off into space. They're running reels through their minds, telling themselves stories. Daydreaming, fantasizing. *What if . . . when I . . . someday I'll . . . wouldn't it be great if. . . .*

Stories are what we human beings feed on emotionally and psychologically. Stories explain the world to us in a personal, feeling way. All the great myths are stories that explained the world to people whose information was far less than our own. Now we have fabulous amounts of information. We know about nerve regeneration, black holes, quasars, white dwarfs . . . yet we still crave stories. We are creatures of curiosity. We want to know about other creatures like ourselves, and we can't possibly satisfy that curiosity without reading: novels, stories, true stories and fictional stories.

We come out of ourselves when we read. We reach beyond our smallness and into the great world. And this we need to do more today than ever before. We all need each other now, more than we ever have. We need each other to save our world, our planet. We need to understand others, to take them into our lives and ourselves. The greatest gift you can give your students is a love of reading. Reach down, hold out that ice-cream cone . . .

Stories can help teenagers look at their feelings, or come to emotional resolution, from a safe distance. If, as an author, I can make an emotional connection with my reader, I have already started to help him or her heal.

4

Healing Through Literature

Chris Crutcher

IT'S a tough requirement, but so far they've all met it. Before a major protagonist is released from a Chris Crutcher novel, he or she must demonstrate mastery of one concept: *Things have been misnamed.* I don't consciously set out with that in mind, but without conflict there is no story and the real conflicts in teenagers' lives often result from what seem like glaring inconsistencies created by adult expectations.

Louie Banks in *Running Loose* has grown up believing that life is fair; that adults don't lie, that if you work hard you get what you deserve, that good intentions count, that disappointments can be overcome by hard work, that his parents and teachers and coaches have his best interest at heart. Then his coach asks him to play dirty football and, though Louie refuses, he sees that cheaters *do* sometimes win—at least in the sense he has always considered winning. Lies *work.* When he loses his girlfriend senselessly in an automobile accident, he learns that not only are *people* not fair, *life* is not fair. After several futile attempts to right the wrongs that have befallen him, in which he makes his situation worse by multiples of ten, he sits, beaten, in the dim light of his grizzled old friend Dakota's tavern, hours after closing, desperately trying to get a handle on his life, which is spinning out of control. He has even invoked the Supreme Being, to no avail. "Louie," Dakota says, "it ain't safe."

"What's that?"

". . . School. Football. This here bullshit life. It ain't safe. None of it."

"You're right," I said. "It's a lot of things, but safe ain't one of them. I gotta tell you, Dakota, I don't get it. Man, what did Becky ever do to get killed? What did any of us ever do? It just isn't right."

"Nope," he said. "It ain't right, that's for sure."

I just shook my head, and for only the second time the tears came. And man they came. I must have lost five pounds. Dakota stood there and watched me. "It's just not fair," I said. "What kind of worthless God would let this happen?"

"Louie," he said, "I ain't an educated guy; but I listen pretty good and I see pretty good, and one thing I'm pretty sure of is that if there's a God, that ain't his job. He ain't there to load the dice one way or the other."

I didn't say anything; I didn't get it. Dakota said, "Boy, if you come through this, you'll be a man. There's one thing that separates a man from a boy, the way I see it, and it ain't age. It's seein' how life works, so you don't get surprised all the time and kicked in the butt. It's knowin' the rules."

"The rules," I said. "How can you know the damn rules? They keep changing."

"Naw they don't," he said. "It's just that you have to learn the new ones as you go. That's the hard part. Learnin' the new rules when they show theirselves. You go on blamin' God, you get no place. You got to pay attention to how things work. Ya got to understand that the reason some things happen is just because they happen. That ain't a good reason, but that's it. You put enough cars and trucks and motorcycles on the road, and some of 'em gonna run into each other. Not certain ones neither. Just the ones that do. This life ain't partial, boy."

Dakota then plays several games of checkers with Louie in which he alters the rules such that they are simple and easy and Louie can win every time. Louie becomes quickly bored, and Dakota feigns surprise. He can't understand why, he says, if the rules are simple and easy and Louie can win every time with no effort, he isn't having a good time. A light switches on above Louie's head.

As I started out the door, he stopped me. "Louie."

"Yeah?"

"If you was walkin' in the middle of the road an' you saw

a big ol' truck comin' right at ya, you wouldn't stop and ask the Lord to get you out of the way, would ya?"

"No," I said. "I'd probably just get off the road."

"Well then, don't be goin' askin' Him to get ya out of the way of all the other crap that's comin' at ya." He held up his hook and looked at it. "You go on an' take care of it yourself."

In *The Crazy Horse Electric Game* Willie Weaver hears the same lesson. He wants to know why, if life is fair—if there's a God—he was crippled in a water-skiing accident, robbing him of physical gifts that few are ever handed in the first place.

[Lisa] sits in the doorway of her car, pulling off her shoes. "What would be different if you knew why, Willie? You'd still be crippled."

"I know, but . . . if there's a reason; a purpose."

"I'm going to do you a favor. I'm going to tell you why."

Willie waits expectantly.

"You crippled yourself because you stretched the rules 'til they broke. Simple as that."

Willie knows her line of thinking; it's a little like Cyril's, only further out. "But if there's a God . . . I mean, I . . . didn't do anything . . . so bad."

"To have him cripple you?"

"Yeah."

"God didn't cripple you, Willie. You did. You stretched the rules 'til they broke; had to go a little faster than you could, push out there at the edge because you thought nothing could hurt you. You said that yourself."

"But . . . I didn't know."

"The rules don't slack off for naivete," Lisa says. "Physics doesn't work on a sliding scale. You broke the rules, you got hurt." She nods a big nod. "So, now that you know why, how does that help?"

Willie shakes his head. "It doesn't."

"Might as well quit asking, then."

These are not resolutions, but they are tools these characters need to find resolutions to go on with their lives. Why didn't Louie and Willie already know this? Because in an effort to keep children from the pain of living—and in an effort to control them—we tell them lies. Like spankings and threats, lies work immediately. Like spankings and threats, they don't work in the long run, because everyone invariably runs into situations in which what they've been told for the sake of expedience simply doesn't hold up in the real world.

One of the most ferocious enemies of any teenager is power-lessness. Developmentally they are in a time of separation—getting ready to become adults. However, this culture draws that process out for as many as eight years. As a teenager, I am expected to pretend I am an adult, to be polite, to hide my feelings, though I am accorded few privileges that go with adulthood. I'm caught. My parents need to have power over me to keep me from doing incredibly ridiculous things that could damage me for life. My teachers need to keep me under control because they have twenty-five to thirty-five students before them, any one of whom would be more than happy to send the room spinning into total chaos. I may be studying things I'm not interested in, and am often told how important those things will be in my life, when I *know* that isn't true. Nothing seems under my control. Sexually I'm exploding like desert flowers following a flash flood, at the same time I'm being told only to keep it under control, not *how* to keep it under control. I don't know whether it excites me or terrifies me more.

My separation, likely as not, appears in the form of rebellion. I am surrounded by people who are afraid that rebellion will get out of hand, and I can't talk about the fact that I'm afraid because my psyche is far too fragile to take that chance. I don't ask good questions and I don't get good answers. Because of the beliefs of many adults around me, I have confused respect with fear; sex or dependence or addiction or guilt, with love. I have been told I need to be less selfish, when, in truth, I need to be exactly as selfish as I am. I am told to think of others before I think of myself, which is a developmental impossibility. I have been told that some of my best traits, ones that include my as yet unpolished senses of humor and creativity, are unacceptable. In other words, many of the traits that will take me far in later life may be seen as threats to the people who are trying to help me become "responsible."

So here I sit.

A dozen escape routes are available to me—the most seductive, and dangerous, being drugs or alcohol. I can get away from my confusion, my depression, that spinning out of control feeling, simply by taking one of these, or drinking a little of this.

So tell us something new, Chris Crutcher.

No can do. There isn't anything new. However, some of the old things, used in a different way, may help.

Sometime in 1987 I received a letter from a woman who told me she had experienced a stillbirth several years back and had not been able to properly grieve for her loss until she read *Running Loose*, where Louie Banks was able to put words to her feelings, and Dakota came up with what she considered sensible advice for the difficult process of accepting what is and moving on.

Two years ago in Houston, Texas, a girl approached me after I'd addressed her high school English class and said, in strained, halting sentences, that Willie Weaver's classmates treated him exactly the same as her classmates treated her after a crippling motorcycle accident—and that his responses to that treatment were the same as hers. Shortly after she read *The Crazy Horse Electric Game* she talked about her feelings for the first time since her accident months before. To a writer, at least to *this* writer, that's better reinforcement than a huge advance.

A Lutheran minister from Colorado wrote to tell me she keeps *Running Loose* on her shelf to help parishioners with their grieving over death.

One of my own clients burst into my office after reading *Chinese Handcuffs* exclaiming, "That's exactly what it's like! That's exactly what it's like! That's what happened to me. I told and nobody believed me and it just got worse and worse and worse. They said it was my fault."

A maintenance man from a school district in southern California wrote to say that, though the stories were different, his feelings about his life mirrored Willie Weaver's at his most hopeless.

Those are some of the memorable letters, and I'm proud of every one of them. Scores of others point to bits and pieces of all my books, from family abusive issues to the athletic experience to the frustrations of falling in love with someone who doesn't love you—or someone who does.

The common theme is this: Someone else knows what it feels like to have his or her expectations crushed. Things aren't misnamed only for me, but for others too. I'm not alone. I can survive.

I am a therapist by trade. Before that I was an educator, both in public schools and in a special private school much like OMLC in *The Crazy Horse Electric Game*. I have worked with relatively functional families, and I have worked with hopelessly dysfunctional families. Currently, about ninety percent of my time is spent working with victims and perpetrators of family abuse. All the adolescents I have worked with have one thing in common: they are afraid to talk about their fears and their pain. They will show anger or comedy or indifference the entire decade of their adolescence before they will reveal their pain. Again, to a large degree, that's developmental, but that doesn't make it less painful. The process of separation does not lend itself to much public introspection, a fact that leaves most adolescents with scores of important questions and no one they feel comfortable asking. And so adolescents often seem distant, and that scares us because at a time when they need most to access knowledge, they keep themselves farthest from it.

I believe our human mental health depends largely upon *congruence*: the degree to which each of our interior selves matches the external world. From infancy we are taught to hide or disclaim our feelings. Big boys don't cry. (I heard that one for the first time when I was four.) I'm told I'm not really angry when I am. I'm told I'm not really sad when I am. And when I'm told I'm *not*, and I know I *am*, I start to wonder what's wrong with me. What is this monster inside that keeps being what it's not supposed to be, feeling what it's not supposed to feel?

I'm a young girl. I live in a traditional American family that puts dad at the head and believes *reason* is superior to *emotion*. Reason is heard. Emotion is not. My brothers are taught reason. *I'm* left with emotion. Emotion is not heard. I am not heard. My voice is not important. I am allowed to express, but it means nothing. *Girls are like that.* The core of me wants its place in the universe. The healthy part of me wants to be heard, to be important, but girls are emotional, they're not heard. My emotions are powerful, but they cannot get out. I begin to hate myself for them. I get depressed. I feel hopeless and I feel alone.

I'm a young boy. I am told the part of me that feels should not be expressed. I shouldn't cry, I shouldn't pout. I shouldn't be sad. These are the best years of my life. (How's that to set up hopelessness?)

These are but a few examples of what contribute to various states of distress that boys and girls feel as teenagers. By the age of thirteen, I have had these incongruencies with me a *long* time. I am fragile but my fragility must be hidden along with the other *bad* parts of me, because above all, I must look good—and to look good when I feel bad, I have to appear as if I don't care. I have to live a lie.

I don't have cures for these woes, other than to give us adults a big *whop!* on the head anytime we pump incorrect information into kids' heads. That would be impossible to do because we would fight forever over who gets the right to perform the whop! and who gets whopped.

I believe stories can help.

Stories can help teenagers look at their feelings, or come to emotional resolution, from a safe distance. If, as an author, I can make an emotional connection with my reader, I have already started to help him or her heal. I have never met a depressed person, or an anxious person, or a fearful person who was not encouraged by the knowledge that others feel the same way they do. *I am not alone* is powerful medicine. If others feel this way, and they have survived, then I can survive too.

As an adolescent I would rather have hot tar poured up my nostrils than talk about my pain. But if I can consider someone else's pain and it is the same as mine, I can begin to work things out. If I can cry at a movie or reading a book when I can't cry about my own life, I will begin to get in touch with ways to deal with the losses, which is what this is all about.

In a soon-to-be-published novel called *I Am Three*, Terry Davis' main character talks about "The Worst Thing That Ever Happened to Me." The worst thing that ever happened to Bert Bowden could have been any number of traumas we find in literature for teenagers—loss of love, loss of significant others, loss of virginity, you name it. But it isn't. The worst thing that ever happened to Bert Bowden was his loss of dignity. Bert's fourth-grade teacher, with the blessings of Bert's parents, and enlisting help from the other students in his class, broke Bert's will. Bert is a bright, curious kid. He finds joy in learning and in taking on physical challenges. But he is also impulsive. He can't get his hand in the air before the answer tumbles out of his mouth, and he's awfully quick with his sense of humor, which is quite sophisticated. Bert's teacher encourages his classmates to "help Bert past" his problem by pointing out anytime they think Bert is "acting like he's better than anyone else," defined as anytime he impulsively calls out an answer or makes a funny statement. The kids buy into the teacher's game and, before long, Bert is so gun shy he answers no questions in class and basically stops trying to excel, his confidence having dropped off the scale.

His teacher took the best parts of Bert Bowden—his sense of humor, his curiosity, his sense of wonder—and trashed them; held them up for ridicule, and *misnamed* them. He called them *egotism, selfishness.* He told Bert Bowden the good things inside him were bad. There is a monster in you, Bert, and the monster is you.

I think there will be hundreds of kids who will read Terry Davis's story and find seeds for their redemption. Davis does not portray this teacher as malevolent, but rather as a man trying to do his best, given his beliefs. That does not lessen the damage to Bert's spirit. If the two or three broken students in each high school class that reads this book make the connection between Bert's life and their own, Terry Davis has done them a great service. He has not preached to them, has not inflicted his—or Bert Bowden's—will upon them. He has simply shown them another truth. Within that truth—with a small *t*—lies the help.

There are scores and scores of good examples in literature, from Holden Caulfield's sense of isolation to Louie Bank's sense of injustice and despair to Gail's (from Richard Peck's *Are You in The House Alone?*) sense of powerlessness to Ozzie's (from Robert Cormier's *Fade*) sense of rage. Stories don't need a perfect resolution —one seldom exists in real life—to become a tool in the healing process. But there is something they do need. They need adults with the courage to bring them to kids, to be willing to talk about the tough problems they portray, and to refrain from sugar coating them, telling kids things will be all right. Maybe things will and maybe things won't. But there's a lot better chance they will if they are brought into the light of day and confronted and explored and demystified.

Photo by Dr. Esther K. Sleator

Good science fiction not only can teach us a great deal about real science, while at the same time telling an entertaining story, but also provides a vantage point from which we can look with special insight at our own lives and society.

5

Chaos, Strange Attractors, and Other Peculiarities in the English Classroom

William Sleator

CONSIDER, if you will, a place called Execution Square, where we have what seems, at first, to be a very lifelike statue of a monstrous animal devouring a man. But it's not a statue, it's real —it's just happening very, very slowly.

Imagine a little shed in rural Illinois, in which time contracts. Step inside and stay for an hour; when you emerge, only one second will have gone by outside. Now think of a vast, man-made planet where tremendous profit is made from illegal child labor. Or an intelligent race that is almost human, except that it consists of only one sex. Or a society in which human beings are mass-produced on an assembly line. Or the very real possibility of a cylindrical body of water: standing on the deck of a boat, you can look up— and see another boat sailing upside down far above you. And what would happen if a man inherited a time belt? He could travel to tomorrow and become best friends with his one-day-older self and eventually set up a house in 1999 in which a continual large party is going on. People are drinking, playing cards, laughing, dying— and they are all himself. Where are all these crazy things happening?

Science fiction—which from now on I'll refer to as SF—has

tremendous appeal for young audiences. Nobody has to think very hard to make an instant list of hit movies, TV shows, comic books, games, and so on that fall into the SF category. Obviously, SF can be a powerful tool for attracting students to reading. Unfortunately, many teachers are ignorant about SF literature, often contemptuous of it, sometimes even intimidated by it. I'd like to try to demystify SF, correct some common misconceptions, and make a few suggestions about how to approach SF in the classroom.

But first I want to point out that many of the well-known SF books I'll be mentioning are not young adult books; they were written and published for the adult market. Teenagers read and enjoy them—some of the most devoted SF fans are in their teens. Unfortunately, many of these fans don't know that there are also authors who *do* write SF specifically for young adults, people like H.M. Hoover, Monica Hughes, Peter Dickinson, John Christopher, Bruce Coville, and myself, among others. I'm not familiar with all of them, I'm not an authority on young adult SF literature, I just write it. But I urge you to check out lists of recommended SF titles for young adults, put out by the American Library Association and other organizations. Young adult SF books are of dependably higher quality than the banal and indistinguishable mass-market paperbacks that flood the shelves.

What is SF? My own definition is that it is literature about something that hasn't happened yet but might be possible some day. That it might be possible is what separates SF from fantasy—and also why it has such appeal for young readers. Only in this genre can you have your cake and eat it too. All sorts of magical, dreamlike things can happen, and at the same time you can really believe in them.

In fantasy we are asked to believe in wizards, ghosts, and magic spells—and most teenagers know these things don't exist. In SF we are asked to believe in robots, other planets, super-computers —all of which *do* exist. Even speculative SF, involving aliens, for instance, has built-in credibility: no scientist can deny the real possibility of alien civilizations. SF confronts teenage skepticism and demolishes it. It's highly imaginative literature that adolescents can really put themselves into, as exciting to the skeptics as to the romantics.

It might seem that my definition—that SF is about things that might be possible—falls apart when it comes to time travel. Time travel is always considered to be SF, yet it is out of the question scientifically. Or is it? Now it turns out that time travel might actually be possible, because of objects known as spinning black holes. That's one of the things I love the most about science—the more scientists find out about the universe, the more weird and bizarre the universe turns out to be.

But why are so many adults convinced they won't enjoy SF? There are a couple of reasons for this prejudice. I'd be the last person to deny that a lot of SF is bad literature, just as a lot of mystery, suspense, gothic, romance, and mainstream novels are bad literature. It's only human nature to reject a whole genre after being confronted with one rotten example of it. (All it took to turn me permanently against the Danielle Steel genre—whatever it's called—was to read half a page of one of her books.) And one problem with SF is that, more so than in other fields, the authors' works are regrettably uneven. Just because you enjoyed Arthur C. Clarke's *Childhood's End* or *Rendezvous With Rama* (both highly recommended) doesn't mean you can wade through *Imperial Earth*. Not being able to depend on particular authors can lead to disappointment.

Many people also have a problem with SF because of a literary technique commonly used in the field. Often, in order to make a future or alien culture more convincing and immediate, the author will plunge readers into the middle of it without explaining many terms and situations. Readers must put the clues together and come up with the explanations on their own, as though they were actually experiencing the events firsthand. This can be a very effective technique when the author is careful and consistent, as Orson Scott Card is in *Ender's Game* (a book that I cannot recommend highly enough—especially for teenagers). By deducing the meaning of the term *three*, the reader is rewarded by feeling clever and is also quickly immersed in the society being described. But this indirect technique can also be a source of great confusion when the author is vague or sloppy, or does not supply enough subtle hints. Then the reader feels lost and stupid and gives up too soon.

The solution to these problems is to avoid the books that cause them. Follow your own judgment and instincts. Don't recommend or teach books that you yourself do not enjoy. Believe me, there are plenty of SF books out there that you will like. SF is a broad field containing many subgenres that appeal to almost every taste.

There are classic adventures, like H.G. Wells's *The Time Machine*. There are also the classic socio-political novels—Huxley's *Brave New World*, Orwell's *1984*. H. M. Hoover's more contemporary *Away Is a Strange Place To Be* depicts the horror of child labor. There are technological mind-benders, once again Clarke's *Rendezvous with Rama*, in which there is hardly any plot, just one more utterly believable (and easily understood) wonder after another. There are superbly imaginative novels of human/alien contact, such as Frederik Pohl's *Gateway* series, and his witty and amazing *Narabedla Ltd*. Ursula K. LeGuin's *The Left Hand of Darkness* depicts a single-sexed alien race whose biology has telling implications about the gender relations of our own species. And there is the relatively new cyberpunk genre, for those who like their reading grittily realistic, exemplified by William Gibson's *Neuromancer*.

All of these books are riveting; they also have a lot more to them than mere adventure or wild speculation. Good SF not only can teach us a great deal about real science, while at the same time telling an entertaining story, but also provides a vantage point from which we can look with special insight at our own lives and society.

Assuming you have the freedom to choose which books you teach, then what do you look for in a work of SF that will make it a rewarding educational experience? I've already made the obvious point that, ideally, it is better to teach a book you enjoy yourself. Beyond that, there are some specific criteria that can help you choose.

First, of course, look for a good story. Extraneous behavioral reinforcers such as grades, stars, point systems, and M&M's have their function. But the most effective way to get kids into reading is to present them with books that are so much fun to read that the reading itself is its own powerful reward. SF has many such books, especially those by YA authors. Look for stories that move quickly, without long, tedious explanations or philosophical digressions. *Eva*, by Peter Dickinson, is an exciting novel in which the many levels of meaning are implicit in the mind-boggling (and totally credible) story. Look for chapters that end at cliff-hanging moments, so that the reader won't want to put the book down, such as *This Time of Darkness* by H.M. Hoover. Look for plots in which information is carefully doled out so that puzzles and mysteries continue until very close to the end, and the reader is compelled to finish the book. *Devil on My Back*, by Monica Hughes, is an excellent example.

Find books with characters and situations that your own students can relate to. There are plenty of SF books (such as mine) in which the characters wrestle with the universal emotional conflicts of sibling rivalry (*Ender's Game*, by Orson Scott Card), peer pressure (*The Boy Who Reversed Himself* by William Sleator), and the generation gap (*The Lost Star* by H.M. Hoover). If a book takes place in the future or on another planet, then it is all the more important that it also deal with familiar issues teenagers can identify with. When some aspects of a story require suspension of disbelief, then other aspects, such as characterization, must be especially realistic to make for credibility.

Lack of credibility is one of the hallmarks of bad SF and fantasy. Characters and settings may be unearthly and outlandish, but in a good book they will also be consistent and follow their own logical rules. The author can't just throw in anything for effect, or make it up as he or she goes along. Aliens or inhabitants of the future must have clear and understandable motivation for what they do; it may not be immediately apparent, but it must become so eventually. Without good reasons for the way exotic societies are structured, nobody—especially teenagers—will believe in them.

The Chrysalids, by the British author John Wyndham, contains an excellent example of an imaginary yet inevitably plausible society. The book takes place after a nuclear holocaust; radiation has caused numerous and continuing mutations in plants, animals, and humans. Those people who have survived without mutation have developed a brutal fundamentalist religion, the goal of which is to preserve the species as they believe God intended them to be. Mutant plants and animals, called abominations, are destroyed. Mutant human beings, no matter how insignificant their deviation from the norm, are labeled blasphemies and sent to live in the wilderness of the Fringes, areas where plant life has been severely mutated.

The structure and belief system of this society are a logical result of the effects of radiation and are also consistent with human behavior as we experience it. Hatred and fear of those different from ourselves is a normal human trait. For these reasons the book has inherent and undeniable credibility. We also feel the horror on an emotional level, because the protagonist himself is a deviation. He and a small group of others have mental telepathy and live in constant danger of being discovered. Because of the action and suspense, teenagers will find the story highly entertaining. (I adored this book when I was thirteen.) They will also come to understand what it feels like to be different, and a victim of intolerance. This book could easily be a stimulus for class discussions on many subjects.

All the guidelines I've mentioned can be applied to fantasy as well as SF. The element unique to SF is, of course, science. Science is the ultimate reality. It's fact. And the story possibilities it provides are endless. Gravity really does slow down time, meaning time goes faster for astronauts in weightless orbit around the earth; when they return, their watches are ahead of earth watches. In biology, physiology, engineering, and many other fields, an intricate process known as period doubling leads inevitably to chaos. And according to a new theory in physics, the superstring theory, there really are ten spacial dimensions in the universe. Once SF authors have a scientific principle going for them, they can then slyly stretch it beyond the limits of reality without the reader being aware of it. SF takes scientific laws—which have built-in credibility—and uses them to make almost anything possible.

In one of my own books, *House of Stairs*, the principles of operant conditioning, as described in rigorous scientific studies by B.F. Skinner, determine the structure of the plot. Five teenagers are locked up without explanation in an environment of endless stairways. Their only sustenance is provided by a machine that emits pellets of food through a slot. They soon learn that the machine will feed them only if they follow certain clearly defined and ultimately nightmarish rules of behavior.

What makes it possible to believe in this scenario is that the machine operates strictly on a schedule known as variable ratio reinforcement. Reader's don't need to know the name of the schedule; they don't need to know that variable ratio reinforcement has been proven to be very powerful at controlling behavior. Simply sticking to this schedule gives the story an inherent, common-sense logic that would be missing if I had been vague or sloppy about the rules of operant conditioning. My main motivation in using science was to give the story credibility. But being careful about the science also has a satisfying side effect: any kid reading this book will come away from it with an innate understanding of the principles of conditioning, whether he or she is aware of it or not.

So why not make readers aware of it? One of the most valuable attributes of SF is that it can stimulate intellectual curiosity. An entertaining piece of fiction based on a scientific principle can often arouse a student's interest more effectively than a textbook. I had no particular fascination with astronomy until I read Frederik Pohl's *Gateway*. His fictional treatment of the properties of black holes, the Schwarzchild radius, and the event horizon was what got me going. It was after reading his book that I started asking questions, reading Stephen Hawking, doing the research that finally resulted in my own book about a black hole, *Singularity*. Reading SF leads naturally to expository as well as creative writing projects on a variety of subjects.

The term *nonlinear dynamics* doesn't sound like a whole lot of fun, but mention its synonym *chaos*—a condition teenagers are naturally drawn to—and they may start to listen. I based *Strange Attractors* on the scientific study of chaos, but only about 10 percent of the research I did found its way into the book. After teenagers read it, teachers may be able to prod them into finding out more. Look at pictures of the Mandelbrot set, a gorgeous and endlessly fascinating display. No matter how much it is magnified it remains equally dense and complicated, revealing more flamboyant new patterns—and also continuing to give birth to miniature versions of the entire figure. By studying it, a student may even begin to understand something about complex numbers. Find out about monstrous objects like the Menger sponge, a cube full of holes that has an infinite surface area but no volume. What would it be like to be trapped inside it? Have students think about it and write essays on the subject.

Another attribute of chaotic systems is extreme instability with respect to initial conditions. In dry technical terms this means that a tiny, seemingly insignificant change at the beginning of a process leads to vast differences later on. It also happens to be a precise description of the behavior of taffy pulling machines and French puff pastry. Think about what it says about the weather, and "the butterfly effect"—the fact that a butterfly flapping its wings in India can change the temperature in Chicago a week or so later. And how does this same instability relate to chance and fate in human lives? Say you stay one minute longer at a party. And you meet someone new who has just arrived. Six months later you marry that person. If you'd left the party one minute earlier, the rest of your life would be completely different. This is not fantastic speculation, it is a very real aspect of our lives. Ask students to write about it.

Clifton Fadiman's amazing collection, *Fantasia Mathematica*, contains several marvelous stories about the fourth dimension. Rudy Rucker's witty nonfiction treatment of the subject, *The Fourth Dimension*, makes the concept so clear that even adults may be able to grasp it. Look at computer pictures of four-dimensional objects. What would you do if you could go into the fourth dimension? What would the fifth dimension be like? What kind of beings might live in such an environment?

"Back to the Future" is one of the most popular movies ever made. But it barely scratches the surface of time travel and is not nearly as imaginative or convincing as dozens of SF books on the subject. For a real trip, pick up Heinlein's *The Door into Summer* or David Gerrold's *The Man Who Folded Himself*. (Be sure to read both of these books yourself before recommending them to students.) Then look into the very real and very peculiar properties of time. Time slows down for an object that is accelerating, an effect that has been measured with atomic clocks. The faster you travel, the slower time goes. It's not speculation but actual fact that an astronaut traveling at near light speed could go on a trip that takes him five years, during which time fifty years would pass on the earth. Look at quantum mechanics, which seems to demonstrate that you actually can change the past without creating an impossible paradox. All that will happen is that the universe will split, and there will now be two versions of everything. Encourage students to think about changing the past. Have them write about what this country would be like if we'd lost the revolutionary war. What single event in their own past would they change if they had the chance? What would their life be like now if they did?

What does SF tell us about our own behavior, and our effect on the world? It's true that there are a few works of SF that have made accurate predictions about the future. Jules Verne came up with the idea of the submarine before anyone else did, and also described other gadgets that were later invented. George Orwell's portrayal of a communistic totalitarian regime was not too far off the track—though the original title of his book was *1948*. For the most part, however, SF is too young a field for us to be able to know at this point if most authors' predictions are accurate or not.

But what we *can* see is a general shift in attitudes about what the future will be like. Victorians believed that technology would lead to a Utopian world in which machines would improve the standard of living and do most of the work, freeing people to lead leisurely, carefree lives. This attitude began to change around the time of World War I, when technology no longer seemed so benign. Authors' predictions became pessimistic. E.M. Forster's story, "The Machine Stops," offers one of the bleakest views of man's dependence on machinery. He describes a future in which people have lost interest in the natural world (the surface of the earth is too polluted for human habitation in any case) and everyone lives in individual cells inside an underground machine. People have no direct contact, rarely leaving their cells; they speak to each other only through the machine, which also provides them with entertainment, clothing, food, and air. No wonder the characters are upset when the machine breaks down. (I can understand their dismay; I feel exactly the same way about my computer.)

But SF isn't only about the future. It gives us a particular perspective on the human condition, in a way that is unique. Realistic fiction is limited to depicting the behavior of only one intelligent species, on one world, with which we are already somewhat familiar. SF has the freedom to imagine the development of intelligence under vastly different conditions, in many environments, and to describe the relations between humans and non-humans. How would we appear to thinking creatures who evolved from insects? How would they treat us? And how would we treat them? Most of us have little empathy for other human beings, only minimally different from ourselves. How much more empathy would be necessary for us even to begin to try to understand physically repulsive creatures from another world? One of the most outstanding recent books on the subject is Orson Scott Card's *Speaker for the Dead*, which manages to be tragic as well as ultimately optimistic. Many brilliant and serious authors have addressed the issue of interspecies empathy, and reading their work can't help but stimulate our own tolerance and insight.

And for that reason, I can't think of a better antidote to teenage peer pressure and conformity than SF. As far as I know, no one has done a rigorous, large population double-blind scientific study on teenage SF fans and peer pressure. So what I am about to say is a subjective opinion based on purely anecdotal evidence.

I have met many teenagers who read SF, and they are about as far as you can get from TV-addicted rock-star-worshipping clones. They are a diverse yet open-minded group who seem refreshingly free of the obsession to be exactly like everyone else. I can't *prove* that reading SF made them this way; maybe it's the other way around, and it is that kind of person who is attracted to SF. However it works, I find a definite correlation between reading SF and having the freedom and self-confidence to disregard convention and think for yourself.

Can there be a better reason than that to push SF at teenagers?

Photo by Nadine Edris

If poetry is to do more than furnish answers on a multiple-choice test, we must relate poetry to the real world, finding poems that are connected with something that happened at school or in the community or in the world.

6

The Possibilities of Poetry

Paul B. Janeczko

M ANY people who knew me during those heady days of grammar-school-into-high-school would be shocked to learn that I wound up being a teacher, poet, and poetry anthologist. In those days I had my sights set on more glamorous goals. Among other things, I was interested in being an Edsel salesman, an all-night rock 'n' roll disk jockey, and a baseball player. (I would have settled for being a bullpen catcher.) Poetry meant no more to me than photosynthesis, the Belgian Congo, or flax.

While I wasn't much of a student, I was a keen observer, often bringing up things like, "Did you ever notice that all nuns have good penmanship?" or "Did you ever notice that Ozzie Nelson never goes to work?" One of the things I observed about the poems that we read in school was that they always rhymed. It never occurred to me that poetry didn't have to rhyme. Another observation about poetry was that poems seemed to be written about subjects on the Official Approved List of Subjects You Can Write Poems About. Among the subjects on the list were:

- Tragic Ends
- Pure (but usually broken-hearted) Love
- Courage
- Pets

- Nature (in which natural things are given oddly unnatural qualities)
- Patriotism

It seemed to me that the poems we read were supposed to edify, enlighten, or illuminate. A really good poem would do all three. The problem was that my cronies and I never seemed to "get" the poems, much the way we rarely "got" the solution to a math problem. Poetry only puzzled, intimidated, and infuriated us.

Somehow, and this may be an unsolved mystery worthy of prime-time television, I became a poetry junkie. These days I read poetry the way some people watch soap operas, work in their gardens, or follow the Red Sox: irrationally, compulsively, endlessly. I read poems nearly every day whenever I find myself with a few unfilled minutes. In fact, I've discovered some wonderful poems while waiting to have my car repaired, eating breakfast, and sitting out an early April blizzard. I've come to share the feelings of James Dickey: "What you have to realize . . . is that poetry is just naturally the greatest goddamn thing that ever was in the whole universe. If you love it, there's no substitute for it" (*The Craft of Poetry*, ed., William Packard, Doubleday, 1979, p. 151). I love it, and it disturbs me that more kids do not.

In *What Do Our 17-Year-Olds Know?* Diane Ravitch and Chester Finn put us on notice that poetry is "not in high favor" with seventeen-year-olds. (I wonder what things—unrelated to sex, drugs, and rock 'n' roll—seventeen-year-olds *do* hold in "high favor.") Sixty-five percent of girls read poetry on their own, while only 45 percent of boys do. While I don't question these numbers, I have a feeling that these figures are higher than they'd be if we put the same questions to insurance salespersons, bus drivers, accountants, and even school principals. Nevertheless, anyone who's spent any time in a classroom knows the feeling when you announce that the class is about to begin reading or writing poetry. Such an announcement brings out insecurities in many teachers and antagonism (or, if we're lucky, merely disinterest) in young people.

While Ravitch and Finn have the numbers, I can't help but feel that they asked the wrong questions. Would not a more telling question be: Why do little more than half of the students questioned read poetry on their own? Perhaps the answer lies in the fact that the poetry they are told to read is selected and presented in a way that is intended to prepare them for a standardized test (or a TV game show) or to demonstrate to some adults what kids their age do/don't know, rather than in a way that would allow young people to experience the fire and ice of words. Too many kids are taught to recognize the author of "Song of Myself" and "The Love Song of J. Alfred Prufrock" for a multiple-choice test; not enough kids are given the chance to read a wide range of poems about topics that touch them. I share Anatole Broyard's fear that we don't read enough poetry. "Where will our flair come from," he wrote in the *New York Times Book Review,* "our hyperbole, our mots justes? Unless we read poetry, we'll never have our hearts broken by language, which is an indispensable preliminary to a civilized life."

Any examination of what kids think of poetry must begin with the poetry we use in the classroom. What poetry should we use? Teachers should use only those poems that we are excited about. If we're not engaged by a poem, can we expect more from our kids? Of course, we must temper that enthusiasm with an understanding of our students, but the possibilities are limitless.

Teachers of poetry must first become readers of poetry. Unfortunately, many teachers are intimidated by the poems they find in some magazines and poetry collections. I'm not sure why, but teachers feel they must understand and/or enjoy every poem they read. Many young readers share this same burden. Why should we enjoy every poem we read? Do we enjoy every novel we read? Every song we hear? Why, then, should we feel we need to enjoy (or understand) every poem we read? I've read thousands of poems to find the best to include in my eleven anthologies. If I had enjoyed every poem, my anthologies would have been impossible to put together. We are vulnerable when we're in front of a class sharing poems. We want our audience to like all the poems. They won't. And if they feel that we expect them to like every poem and they find themselves not liking every poem, they may begin to feel inferior or intimidated.

In selecting poems to share with our students, let's not always choose serious poetry. While much good poetry strikes a deep emotional chord, students need to see that poets can be playful as well as pensive, that poets work as hard on humorous poems as they do on serious ones. If you're looking for poems that will make kids chuckle, maybe even laugh out loud, consider the work of these poets: John Ciardi, X. J. Kennedy, Karla Kuskin, Edward Lear, Eve Merriam, Cynthia Rylant, Shel Silverstein, and Paul Zimmer.

If we don't know what kinds of poems the kids like, we can ask them to show us. Raid the school library and your own library for poetry books. Let the kids read through the books—individually or in groups, silently or to each other—in search of poems they like. Perhaps what they find will be the beginning of a poetry notebook or a poetry wall or a poetry corner of their favorites. It certainly will furnish a good starting point to talk about poetry: what it is, why we like what we do, why the poets wrote the way they did, etc.

Let me offer some anthologies that should be available in your school or local library. No doubt you will have others that you'd like to add to the list.

The American Poetry Anthology, Daniel Halpern, ed., Avon.

American Sports Poems, R. R. Knudson and May Swenson, eds., Watts/ Orchard.

Carrying the Darkness: The Poetry of the Vietnam War, W. D. Ehrhart, ed., Texas Tech University Press.

Geography of Poets, Edward Field, ed., Bantam.

Harper's Anthology of Twentieth Century Native American Poetry, Duane Niatum, ed., Harper.

Love Is Like the Lion's Tooth, Frances McCullough, ed., Harper.

The Music of What Happens: Poems That Tell Stories, Paul B. Janeczko, ed., Watts/Orchard.

The New American Poetry, Donald M. Allen, ed., Grove.

Piping Down the Valleys Wild, Nancy Larrick, ed., Delacorte.

The Place My Words Are Looking For: What Poets Say About and Through Their Work, Paul B. Janeczko, ed., Bradbury.

The Poetry of Black America, Arnold Adoff, ed., Harper.

Poetspeak: In Their Work, About Their Work, Paul B. Janeczko, ed., Bradbury.

The Rattle Bag, Seamus Heaney and Ted Hughes, eds., Faber & Faber.

Reflections on a Gift of Watermelon Pickle . . . , Stephen Dunning, Edward Lueders, and Hugh Smith, eds., Lothrop, Lee & Shepard.

Sounds and Silences: Poetry for Now, Richard Peck, ed., Dell.

Under All Silences: Shades of Love, Ruth Gordon, ed., Harper.

The Voice That Is Great Within Us, Hayden Carruth, ed., Bantam.

Another place to look for good poetry is in the books of poets we enjoy reading, poets we've discovered, perhaps in an anthology. Let me offer the names of some poets and their books that are worth sharing with our students.

Jo Carson. *Stories I Ain't Told Nobody Yet.* Watts/Orchard.

Robert Currie. *Yarrow.* Oberon Books.

Robert Francis. *Collected Poems 1936–1976.* University of Massachusetts Press.

Gary Gildner. *Blue Like the Heavens: New and Selected Poems.* University of Pittsburgh Press.

Dana Gioia. *Daily Horoscope.* Graywolf.

David Huddle. *Paper Boy.* University of Pittsburgh Press.

June Jordan. *Naming Our Destiny: New and Selected Poems.* Thunder Mouth.

X. J. Kennedy. *Cross Ties: Selected Poems,* University of Georgia Press.

Ted Kooser. *Sure Signs: New and Selected Poems.* University of Pittsburgh Press.

Maxine Kumin. *Our Ground Time Here Will Be Brief.* Penguin.

Stanley Kunitz. *The Poems of Stanley Kunitz, 1928–1978.* Atlantic.

W. S. Merwin. *Selected Poems.* Atheneum.

Robert Morgan. *At the Edge of the Orchard Country.* Wesleyan University Press.

Naomi Shihab Nye. *Hugging the Jukebox.* Breitenbush.

Linda Pastan. *PM/AM: New and Selected Poems.* Norton.

Marge Piercy. *Circles on the Water: Selected Poems.* Knopf.

Richard Snyder. *Practicing Our Sighs: The Collected Poems.* Ashland Poetry Press.

Gary Soto. *Black Hair.* University of Pittsburgh Press.

William Stafford. *Stories That Could Be True: New and Selected Poems.* Harper.

John Updike. *The Carpentered Hen and Other Tame Creatures.* Knopf.

Paul Zimmer. *Family Reunion: Selected and New Poems.* University of Pittsburgh Press.

It takes creativity and hard work to bring poetry and young readers together. We must not, therefore, proclaim May (or some other month, usually in the spring) as Poetry Month and ignore it the rest of the year. If poetry is to do more than furnish answers on a multiple-choice test, we must relate poetry to the real world, finding poems that are connected with something that happened at school or in the community or in the world. If the poem hits the mark, the kids will see the connection between poetry and their lives. Offer poems about apples in the fall, sports poems in the midst of an exciting season, and funny poems when somebody (the teacher?) needs a laugh. Offer a poem about living any time. Let students feel what Robert Francis meant when he said, "A poem is like an arrow; it's got to wound you." (Robert Francis, *Pot Shots at Poetry*, University of Michigan Press, 1980, p. 8.)

Poems can fit into a lesson any time, which isn't to say that we should use a poem merely as a "filler." But it does mean that we needn't feel compelled to "cover" every poem we share with our students. We should spend more time reading poems aloud and allowing students to read some poems that have moved them. We can ask for a reaction, a comment, or a question on the poem. On some days the poem may lead to a discussion. When that doesn't happen, however, we need not feel defeated. It's important to give students a chance to hear the music of poetry.

Whenever I work on a new anthology, I discover again the possibilities of poetry, and I want to share those possibilities with my readers. Possibilities in form, language, image, structure, rhythm, voice, sound, feeling. I want my readers to see that poems are expressions of human experience, that poems are as different as people. Further, I want young people to understand that the feelings *they* have are shared by many people.

Students need to be shown that good poetry captures the meanings in life, that it communicates through intense, inventive language. One way to present poetry is the way I present it in my anthologies: by topic. In classes, workshops, and anthologies I've offered poems about teeth, suicide, lasagna, movies, swimming, insomnia, gluttons, dentists, war, crows, cars, cats, and gnats. And that's only the beginning of a list that should show kids that the Official Approved List of Subjects You Can Write Poems About can include just about anything. Here are a few sample groupings of poems that have worked with my students:

SPORTS
"Shooting," B. H. Fairchild
"Nothing but Net," Roy Scheele
"The Hummer," William Matthews
FOOD
"Lasagna," X. J. Kennedy.
"Watermelons," Charles Simic
"Celery," Ogden Nash
TEETH
"A Poet's Farewell to His Teeth," William Dickey
"My Teeth," Ed Ochester
"After the Dentist," May Swenson

But the possibilities of poetry don't stop here. We can show teenagers the possibilities of form as they read elegies, parodies, rondeaus and odes, clerihews, haiku, epigrams and epitaphs, concrete poems, found poems, synonym poems, acrostic poems, light verse, blank verse, free verse, lyrics, limericks, and epics, couplets, tercets, and sonnets (Elizabethan and Italian), refrains, and quatrains. And there are more.

I want young people to taste the richness of a good poem. I want them to feel how poems that touch them have a purpose, described well by Jonathan Holden: "to give shape, in a concise and memorable way, to what our lives feel like . . . Poems help us to notice the world more and better and they enable us to share with others." (*Poetspeak: In Their Work, About Their Work*, ed., Paul B. Janeczko, Bradbury Press, 1983, p. 44.) To this end, let me suggest presenting poetry as experience, so students can see that poetry sings of human experiences, very often, their own experiences. Some sample groups are:

OUTCASTS
"Dancing School," Jonathan Holden
"Nightmare," Edward Field
"Blubber Lips," Jim Daniels
FAMILY
"My Mother's Death," Judith Hemschemeyer
"All," Ledna Gom
"When the Ambulance Came," Robert Morgan

LOVE
"Valentine," Donald Hall
"Warmth," Barton Sutter
"For Sue," Philip Hey

YOUTH
"Two Girls," Charles Reznikoff
"The Hero," Robert Graves
"Zimmer's Head Thudding Against the Blackboard," Paul
  Zimmer

ABSENCE
"The World Is Not a Pleasant Place To Be," Nikki Giovanni
"Song for a Departure," Elizabeth Jennings
"Love Letters, Unmailed," Eve Merriam

Another way of presenting poetry is by highlighting the many functions of poetry. Some poems comfort, advise, recall, implore, describe, mourn, warn. Others mesmerize, mock, and mimic. Here are additional suggestions:

SALUTE
"To the Fly in My Drink," David Wagoner
"The Poet's Farewell to His Teeth," William Dickey

CELEBRATE
"Gift," Ed Ochester
"The Gift," Judith Hemschemeyer

COMFORT
"Tomorrow," Mark Strand
"Spring and All," Grace Bauer

NARRATE
"Elevation," Robert Morgan
"The Dog Poisoner," Keith Wilson

FANTASIZE
"House-Hunting," David Wagoner
"On Certain Mornings Everything is Sensual," David Jauss

Such groupings allow the teacher to connect the poems with the themes and issues raised by fiction and nonfiction read in the class. When my ninth graders have finished reading Robert Newton Peck's *A Day No Pigs Would Die*, I might introduce some of these poems:

- "Dog's Death," John Updike
- "A History of Pets," David Huddle
- "Elegy," Howard Nemerov
- "Pa," Leo Dangel
- "Edwin A. Nelms," Sheryl L. Nelms
- "My Mother's Death," Judith Hemschemeyer

In the same way, of course, poems can be used to introduce a theme of the novel or play you are studying. For example, a poem about suicide can lead into a reading of *Tunnel Vision* or *Ordinary People*.

Poems—not definitions, lives of the poets, dates—should be a delicious part of the feast of literature we offer our kids, not brussels sprouts that get shoved to the side of the plate. If we teachers become readers of poetry, our rooms will resonate with the celebration of poetry as students delight in the possibilities of poetry and share their discoveries.

According to Philip Booth, a good poem "makes the world more habitable . . . it stretches not toward mere pleasure, but toward joy." He goes on to say that a poem

> can be full of joy—no, that isn't true—a poem can *reach toward* joy and sometimes touch joy and touch in others, the reader, the joy of being so true to human experience that, however it may seem, it is finally sustaining. [Any good poem] changes the world. It changes the world slightly in favor of being alive and being human. (*New England Book Review/Bread Loaf Quarterly*, Fall 1988, p. 39)

I can't think of a better reason why poetry must be an important part of our lives and the lives of young people.

Photo by Beth Bergman, Sentinel/Enterprise

Censors wish to hand out blueprints for the writer to follow, blueprints that include designs that are safe and secure, that contain no concealed passages, no corners around which surprises or challenges wait.

7

A Book Is Not a House
The Human Side of Censorship

Robert Cormier

WHENEVER the subject of censorship comes up, I don't think first of headlines or heated debates or Letters to the Editor or angry voices. I think instead of a girl in a school on Cape Cod in Massachusetts. She sat every day in the school library while the other members of her class were discussing *The Chocolate War*. Her parents had protested the use of the novel in the classroom and a hearing had been scheduled. Meanwhile, the novel continued to be studied by the students, pending an official hearing. (In some schools, a book is automatically removed from the classroom prior to a hearing.) I think about that girl. Sitting in the library alone while her classmates were back in the classroom. Was she lonely, embarrassed? Did she feel isolated, ostracized? Did some of her classmates pass remarks about her? I don't know if any of this happened, although I suspect it did. I have this suspicion because a classmate of hers wrote to me about her predicament and his letter showed sympathy and concern. It struck me then as it strikes me now that in a tender time of blossoming adolescence, when a teenager wants to belong, to be part of the crowd, part of *something*, this girl sat alone in the library, sentenced there by her parents. I wonder which was more harmful—her isolation or reading the novel. Which brings us to the ironic P.S. in her classmate's letter

to me: the girl had read *The Chocolate War* a year before the controversy and "liked it."

I also think of another girl, a senior in high school in Arizona
who sent me a letter. This is part of what she wrote:

> A couple of weeks ago I was in my school's library and I was
> going to check out and re-read *The Chocolate War* so my mind
> would be refreshed to read the sequel. I couldn't find it, even
> though the library holds some of your other books that I have
> read. I ended up checking it out at the public library.
>
> The next day I asked my English teacher why your book
> wouldn't be in the library because we had just been talking
> about book banning in one of my other classes. My teacher
> said she thought our superintendent had something against
> your book. .
>
> My friend Jenni and myself asked the school librarian what
> books were banned from our library and yours was the only
> one. This was not fair at all so we went and talked to our
> principal who has since read it and TODAY said he is going to
> put it back on the shelf.
>
> No matter what others may say, keep writing because I
> love your books.

I think of those students and I also think of teachers. I think
of a teacher I met at an educational conference in New England.
She told me that her great ambition was to teach *The Chocolate
War*. She said she keeps ordering the book from her department
head but the book never arrives. She suspects that her department
head does not approve of the novel. He says nothing and she says
nothing. She must say nothing because she is a single parent with
two small children. She doesn't have tenure. "I would love to
challenge him but I can't afford to," she told me.

I also think of a band of teachers in a northern Florida town
who were at the center of a censorship controversy over *The Chocolate War* and *I Am The Cheese* and other books. One of the em-
battled teachers went to her mailbox after her English classes one
day and found the following message, composed of words cut out
of magazines:

> "Woe to those who call evil good and good evil
> who put darkness for light
> and light for darkness who put
> bitter for sweet for they have

revoked the law of the lord
for this you all shall die
one by one."

The note then named that teacher, two others, and a television reporter who had written about the banning efforts in that southern town. Later, someone set a fire at the door of the reporter's home. The teachers received other anonymous letters and telephone calls using such words as *atheist* and *lesbian* and *daughter of Satan*. This was in the United States of America, in the twilight years of the twentieth century.

Thomas P. "Tip" O'Neil, Jr., former Speaker of the U.S. House of Representatives, once said: "All politics is local." Censorship also is local, which means that it is personal, affecting individuals before it is taken up as a cause by groups and organizations and becomes the subject of headlines and talk shows and newscasts.

The human aspects are heart-wrenching because they affect people who are particularly vulnerable:

- Parents—like those on Cape Cod—agonizing over their children who face an increasingly hostile and threatening world, parents who sincerely believe that they are protecting their children when they keep them from reading certain books.

- Young people besieged almost daily by invitations that are beguiling and intimidating and possibly destructive, all at the same time.

- Teachers who attempt to lead their students through the cluttered hallways of knowledge and are often strait-jacketed by people who have never entered a classroom and faced twenty or thirty restless, inquiring, and sometimes bored young minds.

- The writer who seeks to capture lightning on paper, clustering words and phrases and figures of speech to bring character and incident to vivid life.

On the bulletin board above my desk is a paragraph taken from an essay by novelist Robert Daley in the August 18, 1990, issue of the *New York Times Book Review*:

The job of a novel at its highest level is to illuminate the human condition. Entertainment is fine and the transference of ideas is nice, too, but the novel, like all art, has as its supreme goal to engage the beholder's emotions, to make him or her laugh and cry and suffer and triumph and—one thing more—understand.

Beautiful, breathtaking words because they describe exactly the kind of novel I try to write in my days and evenings at the typewriter. Whether I succeed or fail is for the beholders to decide, but my struggle is daily and honest, as well as a continuing revelation.

Writing a novel is a subjective occupation, in contrast to, say, building a house, which is completely objective. The builder follows an architect's blueprint, erects walls, installs a ceiling and floor, cabinets and bookshelves. At the end of the day's work, the builder looks at what has been accomplished and pronounces it a room. At the end of the day, the writer isn't sure about what has been accomplished. Words on paper, yes, but not in response to a blueprint. All the choices that were made. What to put in and what to leave out. This adjective or that. Or no adjective at all. Did this metaphor go askew, calling attention to itself? And the characters: did they come alive? Even when the writer is satisfied with the work and pronounces it, somewhat tentatively, a chapter, there is always the judgment of the reader, the beholder waiting.

This is what writing is all about—the sweaty work of creation, the frustrating and sometimes painful putting down of words on paper to move and excite the reader.

And into all of this stomps censorship, flexing its muscles.

Censorship tells us what to write and how to write it. Or what not to write. Does not trust the motives of the writer. Does not acknowledge the toil that goes into the writing of a book. Blunts the sharp thrust of creativity and, in fact, is afraid of it. Wants everything simple. Wants everyone in a book to live happily ever after.

Censorship goes beyond the writer, of course, to the reader, particularly children. Doesn't want children to read a paragraph that may make them pause and think. Doesn't want children to be challenged.

Censorship sees danger everywhere:

- *Goldilocks* was banned because Goldilocks was not punished for breaking into the house of the three bears.
- Anne Frank's *Diary Of A Young Girl* was removed from schools

because a passage in the book suggested that all religions are equal.

- *The Chocolate War* is banned because of teenage attitudes and because the good guy loses in the end.

Censors wish to hand out blueprints for the writer to follow, blueprints that include designs that are safe and secure, that contain no concealed passages, no corners around which surprises or challenges wait. A house, in which every room is furnished with the bare necessities, with no shadows, no closets, no hidden corners. And no light.

But a book is not a house.

My writing has always been a learning experience, and each time that I sit down at the typewriter I learn something about my craft and also about myself.

I have learned, astonishingly, that not all censorship is bad and that, in fact, censorship for the writer begins at home. At the typewriter or the word processor.

This is what angers me most about censorship, the fact that I have already been censored—and willingly—before my manuscripts leave my house.

I am that censor.

And I've learned my lessons well.

Ironically, I learned about self-censorship long before any of my novels became targets for the book-banners. My education occurred in the final stages of writing the novel that was to become *The Chocolate War*. The novel, which was published in the spring of 1974, was written in 1971 and 1972, long before censorship of young adult books became virtually an everyday affair.

What happened is this:

The events in the novel were nearing a climax and I felt it necessary to include a scene to explain how the villain, Archie Costello, comes upon the idea for a unique but very cruel raffle of those chocolates that are the heart of the novel.

The scene I wrote shows Archie alone in his bedroom, masturbating. He is also disturbed and frustrated about what has been happening at Trinity High School and knows he must bring about a climax to the situation. The scene provides two climaxes—the consummation of that solitary act and the birth of the chocolate raffle. The language was not graphic. There were no four-letter words. But there would also be no doubt in the reader's mind about what Archie Costello was doing. Reading and rereading that chapter, pencil poised to cut or slash, I was satisfied that the scene was cleverly written, showed the connection between sex and power, and, hopefully, captured that forlorn and sometimes desperate act.

My high school son, Peter, had been my guide throughout the writing of the novel, advising me about current adolescent language, customs, styles. Writing the novel had been an exhilarating experience for me. I wrote with all the craft I could summon. More than craft, passion. I was emotionally involved with the characters and events, although I wondered, as I wrote, who would ever read this strange novel about high school students involved in a candy sale. I did not know at that time about the young adult audience, did not know that such a market existed. All I knew was that the novel rang true to me.

At one point, before I submitted the novel for publication, my daughter, Chris, then fifteen, asked to read it. Not an unusual request, because my wife and my children who were old enough always read my short stories and novels in manuscript form. But this time I hesitated. And knew why I hesitated: the chapter showing Archie alone in his room. I did not want her to read this chapter. A solution presented itself. I simply removed that chapter from the manuscript, warned her that she might find a gap in the action late in the novel but not to worry about it, and handed her the manuscript. She read the novel, gave it her enthusiastic approval, and said, incidentally, that she had not noticed any gap.

Off the manuscript went—that troubling chapter restored—to my agent and subsequently to four publishers, who did not care to publish the book. Not unless the "downbeat" or unhappy ending was changed. I refused to change the ending, not so much from noble impulses, but because I simply did not want to rewrite the book. I felt that to have a happy ending the entire novel would have to be rewritten and its flow of character and events altered to make that happy ending logical.

Eventually, the novel was accepted by Fabio Coen at Pantheon Books. He did not protest the unhappy ending, thought it logical and inevitable, given the circumstances of the novel. In a friendly conference in his office, he made a few editing suggestions—so few that they were scribbled on a scrap of paper. Finally, however, he paused, obviously troubled. He said that he had one major reservation about the novel, a certain chapter that was well written and clever—too clever, perhaps—and also gratuitous and out of character with the rest of the book. My mind made a sudden leap— did he mean that chapter in which Archie masturbated? Exactly, he said, suggesting that I reread the chapter once more in the context of the entire novel. He said he would ultimately abide by my decision.

I didn't need to read the chapter again—although I did, to fulfill my obligation. I knew instantly what I had done: I had been willing to inflict that chapter on other people's fifteen-year-old daughters but unwilling to inflict it on my own daughter. I removed the chapter.

That is how I learned the lesson of self-censorship. That censorship begins at home. That a writer works in isolation but is not alone. That cleverness for its own sake is hollow and meaningless. That writing is a two-way partnership between writer and reader.

All of this smacks of compromise, and the danger of being too careful. But it is a compromise that challenges me to my best efforts, that keeps me on my literary toes, that makes me pause with my fingers on the typewriter keys in order to select the perfect word, the perfect simile or metaphor, the perfect motion in a story. Perfection is seldom achieved, but striving for it is, I think, a noble occupation.

The story never ends.

And the battle is never over.

Fifteen years after *The Chocolate War* was written, I sat at the typewriter as usual. Another novel. Another cast of characters. I had embarked on a novel that would eventually be published with the title, *Fade*. Some things never change and among these things are the daily demands of creating characters on the page and setting them in motion.

In this particular novel, a sensitive teenage boy whose name is Paul is the recipient of the gift—or is it a curse?—of becoming invisible. Which, of course, is impossible. Or is it? This kind of enigma intrigues me and made the novel fascinating but difficult to write.

For the purpose of this article, let's suspend disbelief and accept invisibility as entirely possible so that we can focus on one demanding aspect of the novel. The aspect is this: it is necessary for Paul to be shocked by what he sees when he's invisible.

Paul witnesses two unsavory events as he lurks unseen by others: One involves a sordid act between a middle-aged man and a teenage girl. The other involves an act of incest between two young people Paul admires.

Paul must be shocked by what he witnesses, so shocked that he begins to question whether invisibility is indeed the marvelous gift he had envisioned or a terrible burden that he must assume. The scenes must also shock the reader because the reader must share Paul's horror, must feel the revulsion Paul feels.

I wrote the scenes carefully with all the craft I could supply, rewriting as usual, trying to strike the right notes, to convey what was going on in order to make it all seem real. There was also the need to stop short of titillating the reader or sensationalizing the situations.

After the chapters were finished I was left with the eternal questions: Do they work? Would they be convincing to the reader?

Two people whose opinions I value highly read the novel before it was submitted for publication. Both were enthusiastic about it, indicating that the novel had accomplished what I had set out to accomplish. But these two readers also were upset by those two vital scenes. They wondered whether the scenes were written too graphically. "Is it necessary to go into all those details?" one of them asked.

Here again, the writer faces the agony of choice and selection, a question of degree, the delicate balance that must be struck between verisimilitude and exploitation. Was I exploiting the situations, so set on shocking Paul that I had gone overboard? Where do you draw the line?

Rewriting was clearly in order and that is exactly what I did. The younger of the two readers was especially disturbed by the description of incest as witnessed by Paul. I rewrote the scene so that Paul turns away—he can't close his eyes to cut off his view because his eyelids, too, are invisible—and *hears* what is going on rather than sees what is going on. I felt this made the scene less offensive.

In the scene involving the man and the girl, I emphasized the squalidness of the situation, kept the act itself to a minimum. Yet, the act had to be graphically portrayed to justify its purpose in the novel.

The younger reader agreed that I modified the description of the incest but was still bothered by it. Yet, I knew that if she weren't bothered by it, then the scene probably wasn't working. The older reader accepted the scenes as rewritten but without enthusiasm. "I know they're necessary," she said, "but I wish they weren't."

There followed some days of agonizing over the chapters. Some more rewriting and then reaching the point where I felt I could do no more without losing all perspective and compromising myself.

Eliminating that chapter from *The Chocolate War* was, in retrospect, an easy solution. But those scenes in *Fade* remain troublesome for me even to this day. The choices that are really agonizing are those involving *degrees*—how much and how little? And there are no clear-cut guidelines. I have, finally, to be guided by my own instincts.

I have gone into detail about those writing problems to point out that the words that go into books are not chosen gratuitously or casually, that a writer does not press a button and have the words magically appear, that writing is a demanding, exacting occupation. Ah, but when the words sing and dance on the page, when characters leap to life and behave or misbehave, when people read your books and shake their heads and say, yes, this is how life is and how it must be—that is beautiful.

Those parents on Cape Cod continue to haunt me.

I am a parent as well as a writer and I sympathize with them. They acted in what they felt was the best interest of their daughter. They tried to protect her from the world. They had a right to do this, a responsibility to do it, in fact. Who can quarrel with parents who try to shelter their children from what they perceive as bad influences, whether it's a book or friends or strangers on the street?

My wife and I did the same as we ushered our three daughters and son through the frenzied days of childhood and the lacerating time of adolescence, setting up our family rules, our own curfews, our own rules of behavior.

But there's a place where we sharply differed from that Cape Cod family.

Those parents did more than send their daughter away from

the classroom and into the library. They also became part of a movement to censor *The Chocolate War*. They not only did not want their daughter to read the novel. They didn't want anyone else's daughter to read the book, either.

This is censorship in its most basic, purest form.

And this is why censorship is so difficult to fight.

It's the act of sincere, sometimes desperate people who are frightened by the world they live in and in which they are bringing up their children. They are trying to do the impossible, to shield their children from this world, to control what they see and do, what they learn. At a moment when their children are reaching out beyond the boundaries of home and family, they are raising barriers to that reaching out. Instead of preparing them to meet that world, they want them to avert their eyes and remain in impossible exclusion. Beyond that, they insist that this same kind of sheltering be extended to the people next door or down the street or in the next town.

Various organizations—religious and social—are quick to support these parents, and that's when headlines scream across the front pages, voices are raised in anger, picketing begins, and the threat of violence, or even violence itself, erupts.

The supporters of books also have their organizations. Teachers and librarians can turn to organizations within the American Library Association, the National Coalition Against Censorship, the Freedom To Read Foundation, and authors and publishers themselves for help in their battles against the removal of books from libraries and classrooms.

Every writer I know whose books are challenged enters that battle, flies across the country, makes the speeches, debates opponents, offers encouragement to educators who find themselves targets of the book-banners.

I believe, however, that the greatest thing writers can do is simply to keep writing. Writing honestly with all the craft that can be summoned. Writing to illuminate as well as entertain. Writing to challenge the intellect and engage the heart. To make the reader, in Robert Daley's words, laugh and cry and suffer and triumph and understand.

This is what I try to do each day when I sit at the typewriter. This is my best answer to those who would ban my books.

Photo by Don Lewis Photography

The writer's first need is to identify those people who might be willing to read what he or she might be able to write and then to tell them stories that ask questions about their lives.

8

Nobody But a Reader Ever Became a Writer

Richard Peck

BEFORE I was a writer, I was a teacher. I stopped being the one and became the other overnight because there are some bets you can't hedge. It was the night of May 24, 1971. Earlier that day I'd turned in my tenure and attendance book (my first real work of fiction) and found myself, after seventh period, unemployed.

Like a good many English teachers before and since, I was a frustrated writer. In most faculty lounges there's a shadowy figure harboring an unwritten novel, and it's likely to remain that way because teaching is the ideal excuse not to write. It isn't nine-to-five.

I went home from school every afternoon more dead than alive to spend a long evening at the desk, where I still spend the evenings, preparing for tomorrow. There was little scope for dashing off a best-seller or anything long enough to have page numbers when I was either in class or trying to get ready. Teaching expands to fill any vacuum you happen to have. Teachers spend their waking hours trying to turn Life into lesson plans, and summer vacations are mere delusions. After a brief, necessary nervous breakdown, you look up and it's the aptly named Labor Day. Besides, I didn't think I could write. I was standing far too near my future subject matter and my prospective readers to be able to see them.

The English classroom seemed to be as close to the printed word as I'd be allowed to come. But since life is circular, it was teaching that finally made a writer out of me. The writer's first need is to identify those people who might be willing to read what he or she might be able to write and then to tell them stories that ask questions about their lives. The people I wanted to write for were my students. We'd spent years together, and from my first working day I'd learned things about them their parents dare never know.

Semiconsciously, I'd been drawn to the teaching field by the urge to share in the creative process, to teach writing. None of the education courses in college had prepared me for a minute of classroom survival; even a course called "Methods of Teaching English" left me without a single note on inspiring student writing. Grammar wasn't touched on either. I learned grammar during my first year of teaching.

I began by teaching college freshmen English to night-school adults. They needed convincing that they had perceptions worth expressing, that their observations had validity. Then I had to convince them that even though they'd been out of high school for years, they could still find a format for transferring those perceptions onto the page. After a long interlude of high school teaching, I ended my classroom career in the gifted program of a junior high school for girls. My job there was to promote the need for written expression to students who thought that among the Gifted, class discussions were enough.

I came to junior high late in my career and ill-prepared. I hadn't had the pivotal course in all teacher training, "Communicating with the Pubescent," because it doesn't exist. The junior high reading curriculum had always been a problem and continues to be for the teacher who hasn't discovered young adult books. You can get just so much mileage out of "The Red Pony." My search for readings the students couldn't call irrelevant to their immediate experience finally led me to writing young adult novels. Only junior high could have driven me to this extreme. Encouraging their writing was more uphill work. As for competence in grammar, they were a mixed bag. Those from Catholic parochial schools knew some grammar. Those from open-classroom experimental schools had pronounced attention-span problems and had trouble sitting down. Those from public schools were looking everywhere except at me to see who was in charge.

Nobody has yet found a cure for puberty, though, at that time, help was on the way. Judy Blume was in the wings, writing *Are You There God? It's Me, Margaret* to offer aid and comfort to girls passing through puberty, but she didn't publish in time to give any aid and comfort to my curriculum.

Though it wouldn't have surprised an experienced junior high teacher, I was thunderstruck at my students' naked hostility. Very little of it was directed at me. They came in the door bickering and went out quibbling. The only writing they performed with passion was on the notes they tirelessly circulated. Thinking to harness some of this energy, I hit upon a writing assignment that I was altogether too pleased with. One day when they came in bristling, I told them to take out paper, and I dictated the opening line of an in-class composition. It was:

The one thing that really makes me mad is . . .

I told them to fill the page, and they fell to it. That was the first day of complete quiet in my classroom, and I thought I'd lost my hearing. My hopes were high until the end of the day. At home that night, I never quite got beyond the first line of the top paper:

The one thing that really makes me mad is when my mother
talks back to me.

This wasn't the first of my writing ideas that closed out of town, and if there were a foolproof assignment, we'd have heard of it by now. At least this experience cured me of asking them to keep journals.

The flaw in the assignment was that it was writing-as-therapy. Reaching for the undeniably relevant, I'd helped them open a can of worms that was in fact already open. When it came to expressing their emotions, they'd been doing that all along in the circulated notes. We have a bad American habit of encouraging students to do what they're already doing.

Urging the young to express the self and nothing else well before they know anything about the self can lead in downward directions. Expressing anger on the page only leads to more anger, as I've learned at my own typewriter. And one floral, rhymed poem about true love and the pain of parting only leads to another one just like it. "Express yourself" encourages the kind of writing that releases the writer from uncentering in a necessary way. After puberty, it alienates most of the young who have no intention of spilling their sacred secrets on the page.

Writing isn't self-expression. It's communication. In all my teaching I'd avoided the Creative Writing class, the one that says, "Write what you know; reach within yourself for your inspiration." It's a special disservice to those who've taken the Creative Writing course in the hope of becoming professional writers. We don't work that way. We don't write from experience; we write from observation. Our characters regularly find themselves in situations we writers have never experienced and had to go to the library to research. We write every line with our readers' susceptibilities in mind and not our own needs. We write too against the backdrop of continual reading. Writing is work too lonely not to have the inspiration of your colleagues' work, to hear their rhythms and messages. Nobody but a reader ever became a writer, but where is the Creative Writing course that mandates a stiff reading list?

Before I'd been driven to dubious innovation by eighth-graders, I was committed to the idea that reading and writing are two halves of a whole, the one feeding the other. This is a hard concept. In high school it tends to result in a full program of analytical writing to prepare students for what colleges expect. In college-prep courses and certainly in Advanced Placement classes there was no place in the writing program for anything but the critical paper on literary readings—footnoted with any luck. In my teaching years we still expected students to look up the literary opinions of professional critics and to synthesize their findings. Over the years this approach deteriorated into asking students their personal opinions of Henry James and *Hamlet*.

We were always hesitant about asking the young to write a poem in response to a poem read, or a short story of their own ignited by a short story in an anthology. Did we fear that faced with the blazing wit and finish of a Flannery O'Connor short story, our students would be intimidated and experience low self-esteem? Was it safer to watch them cutting Henry James and Shakespeare down to a size they could patronize? Or were our reasons more ominous still: that imaginative writing is hard to grade, or that our students didn't feel like putting themselves on the line?

In that same era, as it happens, a sixteen-year-old girl was going home every evening from high school in Tulsa, Oklahoma, to write her novel, neither encouraged nor impeded by a teacher. She called herself S. E. Hinton, and she called her novel *The Outsiders*, a blockbuster that created a whole new field called young adult books. I don't know the novels she'd read, but she'd clearly read several. She knew that fiction is told by its characters. She knew that paragraphs and chapters and books are shapes. And she wrote from observation, not experience.

The Outsiders is no exercise in self-expression. S. E. Hinton was a girl, but her book is about boys. Like all writers she was a loner, but she wrote exclusively about people in groups. Wisely, she'd ignored any impulse to express her own inner stirrings. Somehow she knew at sixteen what I had to learn at thirty-seven: that novels lie outside ourselves in the world of people around us, and you read many before you write one.

As a teacher, I did what I could to encourage original, imaginative writing that grew in one way or another from our reading. The best writing responses arose from students who wouldn't have gone near the Creative Writing class.

Even with junior high I tried to forge the link between reading and writing, and I carried on the quest for the relevant reading unto the end. In those last pre-young adult book days, I needed a novel for pubescent girls about a girl at puberty. Happily there was a great one: *The Member of the Wedding* by Carson McCullers. Surely the protagonist, Frankie Adams, is still the most telling portrayal of a girl at that age. The novel catches her like a fly in amber and holds her through a static summer. With too much gusto I ordered a class set and handed out the copies one fatal Friday.

On the following Monday they'd all been returned to a pile on my desk. A spokeswoman for the class said, briefly but with authority: "We won't be reading a book about a crazy girl."

I had to give that some thought. Frankie Adams is beset by problems: the angst of being too young and too old all in the same summer. Her body and her emotions betray her at every turn, and everybody in the world has a party to go to but her. She isn't crazy, though. Insanity would have been an escape. She's pitilessly sane.

I read the novel again, trying to see it in the eyes of a fourteen-year-old. It wasn't, of course, written for the young. It was for readers who've made a safe passage to adulthood and dare to look back. It's for readers who know that puberty isn't as endless as it seems. My students had called Frankie crazy because they couldn't distance themselves far enough from her, and she was no one they wanted to be. Worse, the story left her where it found her.

But I wouldn't give up on that book. My memory fades conveniently against how I talked the eighth-graders into reading it. Did I offer unlimited class cuts, money from my own pocket, a party? Probably a party.

Then, pushing my luck, I looked for a writing assignment to complement our reading. By then I knew not to ask them to express their opinions of it. Those who had read all the way to the end were particularly outraged. The novel leaves Frankie Adams suspended still, no nearer an evolution than before. This captures wonderfully the mood of puberty, the mood of the class. I asked them to write alternative endings.

This wasn't my worst assignment. Clearly they thought Carson McCullers needed help. They wrote with a certain verve, tacking on the inevitable unearned happy endings. They gave Frankie what they hoped for themselves: boyfriends and a bust. Most of the stories sent Frankie straight on to Sweet Valley High, though a few existential cynics at the back of the room killed her off. The best papers captured something of the original character's voice, a hint of the strong tone of the novel. One or two papers revealed in their writers an ability for narrative that I hadn't noticed before, and would never have heard in a class discussion.

Wherever I taught and at whatever level, the problem recurred. The young writers didn't have enough vocabulary to write. Of course no student should be admitted to class without a dictionary under one arm and a thesaurus under the other, but that suggests a more orderly universe than ours.

The young in the '90s are manifestly less articulate than previous generations. Few can speak the length of a line without invoking "like" or "you know" and probably both. They are verbally anorexic and getting away with it. This creeping silence of entire generations creates surprisingly little panic in the ranks of teachers.

Early in teaching I learned that you can't instruct the young to vary their vocabulary when they don't have any. The Methods of Teaching English class had stressed that the best way to learn vocabulary is in context. This reckons without the adolescent's ability to skip over any unfamiliar word and keep moving.

I came to my students' rescue here and plucked out vocabulary from their assigned reading. I reintroduced these words on Xeroxed sheets, inevitably causing somebody in the room to ask, "Where do you come up with words like these?" With high school students I stooped lower. When I excised words from their reading assignments, I managed to imply that this vocabulary regularly appeared on SAT tests—which is, of course, possible.

I walked away from teaching in the midst of life, hoping to find another way of communicating with the people I knew best and liked best. I turned to the infant young adult field in the hope that some young people might be willing to read a novel—and then another one—if they suspected it was about them. Or if it was about the people they'd like to be. I exited the classroom to see if I could turn Life into novels instead of lesson plans.

Now I can't remember where I thought I'd find continuing inspiration, voices, plots, and themes away from the living laboratory of the classroom. There's precious little stimulus in the empty room where my typewriter and I live. But as a writer I shortly found myself back in classrooms and libraries, talking with students as the Visiting Author. True, I see them for only an hour of their lives and mine, but we meet in many places, many countries. I catch glimpses of their common threads and some significant differences. I see them moving in a pack, and drifting alone. I hear voices I can't simulate and real-life stories I'll have to tone down for my novels because reality is always too strong for fiction. I hear language I'll have to clean up in deference to parents who will never read my books.

Having been a teacher, I'm more at home in the classroom than anywhere else, but I soon saw that this visiting business needed fine-tuning. At first I went forth in innocence, assuming that teachers who'd troubled to invite me had also managed to assemble a selection of students with questions to ask about reading and writing. Instead, I found myself on the auditorium stage, confronted by an assembly heavy with nonreaders. It wasn't a format for learning from one another. Though you learn more from people's questions than they learn from your answers, they had no questions for me and wouldn't have asked them if they had. It was an exercise in futility. These massed, restless audiences didn't need to see one more adult trying to entertain them. They see that every night on TV and all day in the classrooms of teachers who are far more tired at the end of the day than the students.

My goal was to sit down with a small group to swap ideas, to give readers extra attention and credit since they go to schools where they can't win letter sweaters for literacy. I learned to ask for small groups, and I asked that each participant read at least one of my books as the price of admission.

In most schools this didn't happen. In some places the administration decreed that I must deal with all students or none. In others the teachers clearly had no authority to ask an extra reading of anybody. It was even sometimes suggested that I might magically transform nonreaders into readers by my mere presence. But if students have achieved secondary school as nonreaders, they believe they've whipped the system, and they're lost to us all. Even the idea that students themselves might be expected to conduct our meeting and to write out questions in advance are untried innovations in most places.

Occasionally, too occasionally, it works like a charm. The gathered students expect a lecture from me. I hope for participation from them, and having been a teacher, I'm willing to compromise. I begin and then try to draw them out. Sometimes I read them an early scene of a novel in progress, though I'd never let another adult see it in an unfinished state. Then I ask them how I should end it. Once in a place called Ridgway, Colorado, I read a scene from a novel that became *Close Enough to Touch*.

The opening scene sounds like the closing scene of a romance. A boy has finally worked up the courage to say to his girl, "I love you." She has her reply in readiness: "What took you so long?" The students liked that. Then I said, "You won't see this girl again. She dies, and so the boy has to learn how to deal with his grief, his emotions." They were startled by that, sitting forward. "What do you think he can do to ease his pain?" I asked.

After a silence a boy said, "He could kill himself."

It was a moment when I suddenly didn't want to be there, and I needed words to talk us all away from that terrible solution. I was still looking for them later in a book called *Remembering the Good Times* that dramatizes the classic warning signs of adolescent suicide now that we have an epidemic of it. It was a novel initiated by a boy in a school in Ridgway, Colorado, responding to a question.

Hoping to make every visit count, I've devised a new plan. Now before I accept a school invitation, I ask that all the students

I meet write a paper for me to read before I arrive. This eliminates many invitations, and it limits the meeting to a size that's usually manageable (though I once received eighty papers, UPS, on the eve of my departure).

The paper I ask the young readers to write is entitled "Something That Happened to Me That Would Fit into a Novel." I repeat, there is no foolproof writing assignment, but this one casts a net broad enough to encompass a good, rich range of material. The papers often reveal their writers' expectations for fiction. An assignment is only as good as the teacher assigning it, and so the best of the papers have topics limited and lively enough to treat as single scenes. Often neither students nor teachers appear to have heard of the need to limit a topic until you can deal with it, and the papers cover years of life, hitting high spots and low.

I hope this writing forges a link between the self and the story. I hope it sharpens an eye or two for the material lying near their lives. I hope they see from the papers of their classmates that something really does happen around here.

It's an assignment that might invite self-involved self-expression, but most of the writing is about other people. Often they write about younger children, and there are a lot of deathbed scenes involving grandparents. Some explore sibling rivalry with dialogue that can only be called colorful. None ever touch on the peer-group power structure running their schools because some subjects are too sensitive to treat. In Alaska you get a lot of stories about fish that got away and the night the bear got on the roof; in California a lot about life in the aftermath of parental divorce; and the most popular setting coast-to-coast is the shopping mall. One in a hundred is a comic tale, always written by a boy. One in ten is a hard-to-believe revision of a Harlequin romance, always by a girl. Then there are the people who won't play fair. There are eighth-grade boys who write interminable science fiction. Something that happened to *them* that would fit into a novel? No, but they're in the depths of puberty, and they aren't talking. Stories to them are only for escape, and the farther the better. It's a factor I have to reckon with as a writer for them. I'm moved too to write what they won't: about the peer-grouping that dominates their lives. Their silences are as telling as their words.

Reading their writing before we meet makes everything better.

I catch glimpses of them in advance and try to visualize them. Then when we meet, I ask the author of the paper I thought was the best to read it aloud. Inevitably, it's an outsider.

When our roles are reversed and they are writing for me, it sets up a dialogue. They're no longer the critical consumers that they are at the mall, in front of TV, and in the daily classroom. The very experience of writing something that doesn't go directly to the teacher and nowhere else, a paper that isn't going to be graded, gives the project life.

In one town the PTA was persuaded to publish the papers as a pamphlet to be distributed in the community. This meant that one paper had to be omitted. Because it was about a family trying to cope with the alcoholism of a father, it couldn't be included. But I have hopes for the student who wrote it, who needed to write it, not necessarily as a writer but as a survivor.

Professional writing is the craft of communicating with strangers. However many miles writers travel, we meet most of our readers only through our books. At home, we wait for the mail. Fortunately, letter writing isn't quite dead, even among a generation who no longer need even write thank-you notes for gifts from grandparents. The best letters come from young people who wanted to write them. They often come in the summertime from readers arrested by something in the book that causes them to write back. Often they ask, "Do you live around here?" They little know how encouraging that is, or that adults need encouragement too.

There are those other letters, the ones assigned by a teacher. This often elicits the less stimulating letters: "Our teacher told us to write to our favorite author, and I'm the only one in the room writing to you." Or the other one I've kept pinned on the wall of my study: "Our teacher told us to write to our favorite author. *Could* you get me the address of Danielle Steel?"

The idea of young readers writing to the author is a good one. Sometimes they have questions that the teacher can't be expected to answer. The letter can forge another link. Most people go through life without believing in the reality of writers.

But writing to the author as a class project needs fine-tuning too. Far too many teachers are assigning letters without teaching the format and content of letters. All too often comes the packet of letters with a cover letter from the teacher. The cover letter is meticulous: headed as letters should be, written in ink on unruled paper, even paragraphed. But in it the teacher says, "I'm sending you my students' letters just as they've written them. Please overlook their spelling and grammar."

I can't do that. Spelling and grammar, paragraphing and word choice are the tools of my trade. I live in a real world, one in which spelling counts, and you'd better keep your rough drafts to yourself, whatever you do for a living.

That teacher is a close relative of the one I often meet in school visits. On the topic of composition, the teacher says, "I think they should just *write* without having to worry about mechanics, don't you?"

I don't. I think it's discouraging to write when you aren't learning how. I agree that learning grammar from textbook exercises has its limits, but surely grammar and vocabulary can be taught in a very direct way by using student work. Most teachers aren't so sure about that. I taught points of grammar as they arose, using student-written sentences and paragraphs as examples pro and con.

Being a teacher made a writer out of me. After all teaching is the craft of communicating with strangers in a language you can find. It's the craft of meeting absolute deadlines. It's the craft of trying to give time a shape. These are the needs of the novelist.

I was a teacher as long as I could be, long enough to recognize two built-in impediments to learning in the English classroom. Language as a bond between us all has given way to the teenaged idea that grammar, reading, and the occasional composition assignment are for English majors, and no one else need bother. The noncollege bound don't see high school as their last crack at literacy because we present it for their consideration with no sense of urgency. We even find ourselves reading aloud to them from books written for them to read. Some of the college-bound overlook the hurdle of freshman-year composition, whatever it consists of now, and set their sights on other fields in which handling written, read, and spoken language will either be computer-augmented or you'll have somebody to take care of that for you.

The other impediment that threatens student writing with extinction is the adolescent inability to manage time unaided. Those who work thirty hours a week to support a car, who watch the national average of four to seven hours of television a day, those who are majoring in Something Else can tell us with something like moral indignation that they have no time for homework, let alone written homework.

Adolescence is a passionate belief in short-term gains. Learning to use language so that it won't be used against you is a long-term project, full of lessons that can't be passed off as creative play. Being expected to write only occasionally may be no better than not having to write at all. The occasional writer has to keep starting over from scratch.

Still, the letters come from the literate minority of the young. Quite a number of them want to be writers too, and being young, they want the magic formula, the key that will unlock the publisher's door.

There is no magic formula for anything, but so many of the young write to writers for advice about writing that I've worked up a response to them, and I conclude by sharing it:

TO ASPIRING WRITERS

1. Never write what you know. Write what you can find out. If you're writing research papers that have to be footnoted, you're well on the way to fiction writing because all fiction has to be documented too, on every page in the lives of the readers.

2. Words are the bricks of your writing, and you need a larger supply than you have. If your teachers of all subjects aren't providing specialized vocabulary lists to be memorized, ask them why not.

3. Fiction is strongly based on the search for roots. Most stories are family stories. Take time out from avoiding your parents to find out who they are.

4. Fiction is never about ordinary people. For subject matter, look around for the people in your school who aren't full-time conformists.

5. Write each page at least seven times. Professional writers are just like students: we never get anything right in the first six tries either. If your teachers give grades on rough drafts, ask them to rethink their position.

6. Read a book a week to see how other people do it. Writing is hard enough without the help and inspiration of your fellow writers.

7. Writing requires as much practice as the piano and more than football. Carve out the time from television and spend an hour a day writing.

8. Finally, think of all writing as communication, not self-expression. Nobody in this world wants to read your diary—except your mother.

I believe that it helps for the kids to see me writing along with them and to see my work subjected to the same kind of scrutiny as theirs is.

9

Lit-Lib: Using Literature to Teach Writing

Robin F. Brancato

WHEN I began teaching Creative Writing again recently, after some years of teaching comprehensive English courses to high school students, my overwhelming feeling was of liberation. Liberation from literature? Was this possible? I, admirer of *Antigone*, lover of *Candide*, defender of *A Tale of Two Cities*, I, among the last to abandon *Silas Marner*—and here I was rejoicing, like one of those linebackers in the last row of Required English would rejoice if there were no anthology to lug around, not even a skinny paperback to carry to class. In my case, I was rejoicing at the idea that there was nothing we *had* to read. With all due respect to the generations of dedicated, well-intentioned syllabus-makers who have gone before me, whose choices have shaped me as student, reader, teacher, writer, and human being, I repeat the word *rejoice*. In my two Creative Writing classes I hoped to use as models and as inspiration works that didn't necessarily drag along with them the baggage of the too-familiar title and the look and smell of the bookroom. Our sources, instead, would be anything that fit into my overall thematic plan, with an emphasis on readings that the kids found themselves. Luckily I had the use of a photocopy machine.

The result of this lit-lib approach was that I was kept constantly alert, always looking for new material; the kids were forced to participate in helping to create our "textbook"; and the year's course ended with me as cheerful as I was at the beginning. You'll say, perhaps, that such freedom is impossible to achieve in most English classes, and maybe you'll be right, but a lot of the Creative Writing Approach, as I'll call it, is applicable to other classes. I'm already trying to apply it as much as I can in my remedial writing and comprehensive courses. My two Creative Writing classes happened to be made up of students in grades nine through twelve, combined, in a large suburban high school with an ethnic mix, but I believe that the basic ideas are applicable to the teaching of writing courses or units to almost anyone, anywhere.

I decided to start off the year by giving students a "find list." This was a list of various things I hoped to examine during the course. The list of about twenty-five items included:

- An opening sentence (in fiction) that grabs you.
- A poem you are attracted to but don't understand.
- Ten words you love the sound of.
- Three figures of speech you wish you had written.
- A book that made an impression on you when you were much younger.
- An example of something you wrote five or more years ago.
- A piece of published writing that you think is awful.

My idea was that students could start to be on the lookout for these examples, so that when we were ready to focus on any one of them, they would have had a head start. The list reflected my notion of what the overall shape of the course would be, but I kept adding, whenever one good thing led to another. As you can imagine, some kids were always bringing in examples and others only searched when I gave them a specific assignment, such as:

- Find a definition of poetry that comes from someplace other than the dictionary.
- Find the short story you would most like everyone in the class to read.
- Find a narrative written in a voice that is very different from your own.

If there was a chance that they might not understand what to look for, I showed them examples first. For instance, in order to make a point about the different effects a writer can get by writing a story in the first, second, or third person, I'd show them an example of each, from a collection such as *Connections*, edited by Donald R. Gallo (first person, my own story called "White Chocolate"; second person, "A Reasonable Sum," by Gordon Korman; and third person, "Fairy Tale," by Todd Strasser).

The various items on the find list were to be handed in to me a few days before I intended to use them, so that I could plan an agenda. Sometimes the finds were short enough so that everyone could present his or hers, and sometimes I made choices in order to make particular points, maintain a balance, and keep within the time frame.

Before we get into any more specifics, let me explain my overall concept of the course. I hoped that during and after this experience my kids would:

- Write more than they ever had before, and that they would save what they wrote.
- Read more than they normally took time for.
- Become their own first and best critic and editor.
- Learn to value constructive criticism from others, and learn to give and take such criticism gracefully.
- Observe in a new way and find nothing in life irrelevant.
- Grow enough to reject something they once admired and to admire something they once rejected.
- See reading and writing as lifelong sources of pleasure and comfort.

In addition to these abstract, hard-to-measure goals, I also had a plan regarding what direction we would take and what guideposts there would be along the way. My plan was to have the kids (in approximately this order):

- Look back at their own pasts, beginning with early childhood.
- Look at themselves now.
- Look outside themselves—at people, places, things, and sensations, first close to home and then more distant.

- Look at writers and writing from different times and places.
- Look at the future, from both a cosmic and a personal stand-point.

Within this basic framework I fit the kinds of writing I wanted to be sure not to miss: the first-person narrative (journals, diaries, letters, stories), the poetic prose piece, the poem (structured and loose, short and long, serious and light), the dialogue, the skit and radio play, the short-short story, stories for children, and so on. In addition to these forms, I had students looking for particular techniques and styles (figures of speech and certain verse forms, like haiku). Our usual mode was to begin by looking for examples (from the find list), next examine the findings, and then try our own original pieces, which we shared and critiqued. Whenever we got sidetracked by something fascinating, even if it wasn't in the chronology of the overall plan mentioned before, we went with it.

Let me explain how the kids went about finding things, what they found, and how we used their findings. I urged them to look first in the sources they had close at hand—books (if any) in their homes and magazines they owned or could borrow. Some of them had very few books at home, and for certain find-assignments everybody had to go to the library. I know, now that I've been through this approach, that the kids need time and need guidance in how to look for examples. I eventually built into the course an activity in the library that I called a treasure hunt, but this practice in searching should ideally come early in the year. It doesn't have to be a complete lesson in how to use the library (which they probably get in some other course), but rather a brief tour of literary reference books and, more important, periodic "guided browses" through the books on the shelves, especially the poetry and short fiction, with lots of namedropping of authors they might like. Looking like a bag lady, I also brought books to class for browsing and searching, and from time to time I set up show-and-tell days, when the kids were to bring reading material that they wanted to introduce to the rest of us. A classroom library would have been great, but that wasn't possible because I had no room of my own.

What they brought to class as demonstrations of their taste, and the sources they used when left to their own devices ran the gamut, from the expected teenage magazines and young adult novels to sophisticated pieces by writers such as Emily Dickinson and Jorge

Luis Borges. A lot of what they brought in, even though it wasn't my taste, was just as useful in making certain points as the examples that I would, in the past, have found for them. The obvious difference was that they had more interest in getting the point if the material was theirs. I tried to keep a balance of their finds and my finds, and I tried to avoid repeatedly using the finds of the same students, just as I tried to give everybody equal time when it came to critiquing their original work.

In order to convey a feeling of how the class operated, here is a sampling of what we did.

We started off by thinking of our earliest memories. A good model was the prose poem near the beginning of Richard Wright's *Black Boy*:

> There was the delight I caught in seeing long straight rows of
> red and green vegetables. . . . There was the experience of
> feeling death without dying that came from watching a
> chicken leap about blindly after its neck had been snapped by
> a quick twist of my father's wrist . . .

The kids were asked to find other published memories of childhood in fiction and nonfiction. Then they wrote their own prose poems of childhood, and in addition to discussing the clarity and originality of their images, we talked about the pros and cons of word repetition. (Wright uses "There was . . ." twenty-two times in two pages.) Later in the year, incidentally, at the urging of a visiting poet, Michelle Holland, some of the kids went back to these same early memories to write a piece called "Where I'm From." Others took Holland's assignment less literally and wrote about what has shaped them so far, or about themselves at the end of a genealogical chain. One early-childhood assignment that resulted in very interesting writing was to answer the question "What did you used to pretend when you were little?"

The early-memory prose poems paved the way for a Sense-Experience Week. The idea was that the kids, on designated days, brought in examples of their favorite sights, tastes, sounds, touch-sensations, and smells. Sometimes we turned the exercise into a guessing game. (Close your eyes. What is this sound?) Always, the point was to translate these sensations into words and to try to convey them accurately and without resorting to cliché.

A next step, after the memory poems, was to explore first-person narratives, beginning with those of childhood. Some finds that were particularly interesting were "Celia Behind Me," from Isabel Duggan's *Elizabeth Stories*, sections of Margaret Atwood's *Cat's Eye*, Jamaica Kincaid's *Annie John* (this book is a gem—accessible to students of all ability levels; featuring a girl, but interesting to boys; dealing with a colorful childhood in the West Indies but universal in its concerns; a perfect piece of literature for inspiring kids to write about their own pasts). A lot of first-person narrator finds were from well-known young adult novels such as those of Judy Blume, S.E. Hinton, Paul Zindel, and Rosa Guy, or from other well-known works such as *The Diary of a Young Girl* by Anne Frank or *The Catcher in the Rye*. Some more offbeat finds were *A Boy's Own Story* by Edmund White, *This Boy's Life* by Tobias Wolff, and *A Clockwork Orange* by Anthony Burgess. We didn't read whole books (except in the case of *Annie John*). Usually the students selected a few paragraphs to be photocopied or read aloud, and my hope was that there would be a demand for more than the brief sample. In the case of "Celia Behind Me," for instance, everybody wanted to read the whole thing. Sometimes my dream came true and kids would lend each other books.

What we did with the finds varied from one assignment to another. Some pieces were effective simply when read aloud. Others needed to be reproduced so that they could be seen and analyzed. The kids sensed early on that the effectiveness of a piece often depended on whether it was read well, by a reader whose voice was matched to the material. I encouraged everybody to read, but the kids liked being allowed to choose each other as readers of their finds or their original pieces, and I encouraged that, too. A typical discussion that followed the reading of first-person narratives focused on questions such as What can you tell about the narrator? How old is he or she? Ordinary or sophisticated? Reliable or unreliable as a reporter? How is the author working behind the scenes? How much is revealed and how quickly? What has been left out and why?

At the beginning of our examination of first-person narratives, most of our examples came from short stories or novels. Later we looked at published journals, diaries, and letters and wrote some of our own, both real and fictitious. Finds in this area included *The Color Purple* by Alice Walker, *The Basketball Diaries* by Jim Carroll,

The Adrian Mole Diaries by Sue Townsend (a British best-seller), and *A Book of One's Own* edited by Thomas Mallon. We also examined letters written by slaves during the Civil War period.

There are many variations on journal keeping, but I had the kids keep an ongoing journal that consisted mostly of their responses to questions that we didn't have time to finish discussing in class. (For instance: Have you ever been bullied or been a bully? How important do you think it is to marry someone from the same background as yourself? What is a poem?) Sometimes we shared the responses the next day, and sometimes I let journal entries accumulate, so that I collected them and returned them with written comments that were just between me and the writer. Journals, of course, might also include all kinds of unsolicited entries and notes for future writing projects.

In order to stimulate the kids to remember and use their own pasts, I asked them to bring in children's books they had liked and things that they themselves had written when they were younger. A few students had neither books nor writing samples, but most of them did, and they enjoyed sharing this memorabilia. My impression was that nobody—not even macho eighteen-year-olds—found these trips down Memory Lane to be childish, embarrassing, or boring. In fact, because their enthusiasm ran high for children's books, we used Dr. Seuss and Shel Silverstein as our main models for writing poems with a strict meter, and the kids eventually created their own children's books, some illustrated and in verse and some not. Given my bias toward children's lit, I hauled in a lot of books for them to read and evaluate. In addition to some of the well-known favorites from their pasts, such as Dr. Seuss's *Yertle the Turtle* and *Fox in Socks* (great for a lesson in the sound effects of words) and Sendak's *Where the Wild Things Are*, they were very interested in manners books (*What Do You Say, Dear?* by Sendak, for instance, or the quaint Gellet Burgess books *Goops* and *More Goops*, and other more contemporary examples of how-to-behave books). They also enjoyed discussing contemporary concept books for young readers dealing with such subjects as divorce and nuclear war. The most provocative children's book of all turned out to be *Struwwelpeter*, the classic German collection of cautionary tales by Heinrich Hoffman, found in several English translations. This work in particular got the kids going on the question of whether a young child can be harmed by a book. I found, by the way, that my old favorite,

Winnie the Pooh, wasn't particularly popular in the original, and another favorite of mine, E.B. White's *Stuart Little*, was appreciated only by certain kids.

Other offshoots of children's literature that we explored were fables, tall tales, and nonsense verse. In addition to the obvious examples of fables from Aesop and La Fontaine, the kids responded well to modern fables, such as those of James Thurber in *The Thurber Carnival* (especially "The Little Girl and the Wolf" and "The Very Proper Gander"). They had no trouble at all finding subject matter for their own modern-day cautionary tales and fables. "Jabberwocky" by Lewis Carroll was the obvious choice for introducing nonsense verse, and it, along with *Fox in Sox*, was very useful in making points about the importance of the sounds of words. In connection with the emphasis on sound effects, we examined each other's ten favorite words. Some good original poems and paragraphs came out of using one or more of the favorites. For instance, the word *dovetail*, a favorite of my student Carrie Orapello, resulted in this:

> He worked for hours
> day and night he spent in his workshop
> chiseling
> hammering
> filing
> Finally his masterpiece was complete
> The corners were dovetailed
> a perfect fit
> of course
> Spectacular scenes were carved in
> the sides and legs
> A spotless piece of glass topped it off
> His masterpiece
> made for me

We also played the old dictionary game as a way of calling attention to the connection between the sound and the meanings of words. (I picked a list of funny, odd words from the unabridged dictionary—*kerf, lues, dundrearies, garboil.* The kids invented authentic-sounding definitions for these words, which I read aloud, with the correct definition sneaked in. They guessed which was the real definition. Players got points both for guessing the correct definition and for having their phony one chosen as the right one.) Another book intended for young children that I found useful as we explored figures of speech and the avoidance of cliché was *As: A Surfeit of Similes* by Norton Juster, illustrated by David Small.

In the part of the course where the focus was on the kids looking at (and listening to) themselves in the present, we examined and wrote dialogue. A few of them recorded actual dialogues, and we discussed the differences between real conversation and dramatic dialogue. The samples they chose came more often from stories and novels than from plays, but we read some dramatic fiction together in class from the Scholastic magazine *Literary Cavalcade*, and I showed them screenplays and TV scripts that I had access to. I used models from the Scholastic magazines throughout the course, by the way, especially award-winning pieces by kids their own age, and we routinely read and critiqued relevant pieces of writing from past issues of our school's literary magazine. (In our letter-writing phase I had my kids write letters to the student authors published in our lit magazine.)

When the focus moved to looking-outside-yourself, we looked first at other people and each wrote a character sketch of someone we knew well. I've been saying *we* from the start, because I often did the assignments along with the students. Sometimes I showed what I wrote early on, as a sample, and sometimes I presented mine anonymously or not at all. From time to time I used finds from my own writing, usually with an announcement up front that this was mine. If the piece was something not yet published, I particularly sought their criticism. The matter of how to get kids to be comfortable with and graceful in giving and getting criticism is an essay topic in itself. In short, I believe that it helps for the kids to see me writing along with them and to see my work subjected to the same kind of scrutiny as theirs is. Although it happens that my writing has been published, that isn't very important. The active participation of any teacher, published or not, helps convey the message to kids that *I do this, too. This is important to me. I need reaction from an audience, just as you do, and I have to decide, just as you do, how to use the criticism I get.*

Some other things we did in the looking-outside-yourself phase were 1) to write descriptive pieces based on first-hand observation or inspired by photographs they had taken; 2) to examine the function of conflict in fiction and to write pieces based on various kinds of conflict; and 3) to write about the same incident from different points of view.

When the kids in my classes were given free choice of forms, they usually wrote poems. As may be obvious by now, most of my assignments were tied to ideas or themes, and the kids could decide whether to fulfill the assignment by writing prose, poetry, dialogue, or "other." Off and on, however, we focused on poetry per se and we examined and tried to write various types, from the very controlled (haiku) to free verse, from nonsense to serious, from old style to modern (including song lyrics). One particular collection that yielded interesting finds was *Some Haystacks Don't Even Have Any Needle* compiled by Dunning, Lueders, and Smith. Some other poets, not represented in that collection, whom students found interesting were Emily Dickinson, Countee Cullen, e. e. cummings, Sylvia Plath, Alice Walker, Maya Angelou, Nikki Giovanni, and Rita Dove. Lyrics of the Beatles were popular and inspired some interesting original poetry. Also, a few good poems for raising questions about the nature of poetry are: "How to Eat a Poem" by Eve Merriam, "Literature: The God, Its Ritual" by Merrill Moore, "Your Poem, Man" by Edward Lueders (the last two in *Some Haystacks . . .*), and "Constantly Risking Absurdity" by Lawrence Ferlinghetti. In general, I introduced the terminology of poetry (iambic pentameter, hyperbole, sonnet, onomatopoeia) only when the thing itself appeared and it became convenient to give it a name.

Throughout the course we used examples of writing from widely differing times and places, but the emphasis was usually on the specific poem or chapter rather than on the writer's life or body of work. However, in the part of the course that I thought of as looking-at-writers-from-different-times-and-places, I matched each of the kids up with a writer I thought he or she would like and had them find out about the person's life and work. The kids seemed curious to figure out why I made the particular match. Some of the matches were a bust, but in other cases there was a true marriage. Those who liked what they found made some good presentations to the class. Some of the authors I drew from were: Dorothy Parker, Roald Dahl, Kurt Vonnegut, Woody Allen, Sylvia Plath, Tom Wolfe, Jack Kerouac, Alex Haley, Toni Morrison, Maxine Hong Kingston, Truman Capote, and Agatha Christie.

In the finale of the course we looked at the future, which

consisted mainly of examining fiction in which the world of the future or a surreal world was projected. Several stories we used were: "Button, Button" by Richard Matheson (this story, involving the decision of a married couple whether to push a button that will bring them riches at the expense of the life of a stranger, raises questions about responsibility to others and what it means to truly know your loved ones); "The Weapon" by Fredric Brown (a story in which a stranger tests the ethical responsibility of a scientist); and "X Marks the Pedwalk" by Fritz Leiber (an outrageous science fiction tale in which drivers and pedestrians are pitted in a struggle to the death). One of our "future" activities at the end of the course was for the kids to write letters to themselves, to be mailed to them by me a few days before the start of school next year. Some of them wrote additional letters to themselves, to be mailed when they graduate from high school.

At the end of the course, even though there were unanswered questions, not-quite-finished discussions, and other loose ends, I felt a sense of completion, and I felt more than usual that the students had had a fair share in determining the content and spirit of the course. Although the emphasis was always on their writing (typically at least two days a week were spent in enjoying and critiquing their work), we were introduced to a range of literature, and I profited from their selections as much as they did from mine. I have no scientific way of knowing whether these kids now read and write more than they used to, but I have a hunch that they're inching in that direction.

In conclusion let me mention briefly some of my other feelings and observations about the teaching of writing. I believe that:

- As much leeway should be given as possible when it comes to how assignments are fulfilled. I always gave kids the option of creating their own assignment instead of doing mine.

- As much leeway as possible should be given in terms of allowing free expression, written and oral. We had ongoing discussions about what was appropriate and inappropriate, and I tried to establish an atmosphere in which the only language we completely ruled out was that which was intended to hurt someone. Some of our finds were from works intended for mature readers, but I was lucky enough to have no resistance from students and no problems with censorship from parents or administrators.

- Letter grades should be downplayed as much as possible. I was required to give grades on report cards, but I never put anything except comments on their writing (and then in the form of friendly questions, whenever possible). I told the kids at the beginning of the year that anybody who did all the work would be guaranteed at least a B. There were a lot of A's and B's but also a few failures, in the case of students who missed a lot of assignments.

I tried to vary as much as possible the ways in which their writing was presented and evaluated. I read most pieces in advance before they were used in class (except for some in-class writing that was meant to be spontaneous). Off and on I gave the kids various evaluation forms in the hope that they would come to agree with me about what we were looking for. Sometimes they gave each other oral comments only; sometimes they responded to each other's work in writing—sometimes in signed notes, sometimes anonymously, and sometimes the comments came just from me, either in writing or in a personal conference. I tried to be honest without discouraging kids, and although they sometimes thought I was being stingy with praise, I knew I was also being cautious with negative criticism. When possible, I tried to suit evaluations to each kid's personality rather than to follow a single procedure.

Even though most of the kids ran out of steam after their first straight-from-the-heart drafts, I tried to emphasize the importance of revision. The best way to get them to revise turned out to be a special end-of-the-term assignment. Instead of an exam, they were required to collect examples of their best pieces of work for the term and submit this collection, revised.

In a creative writing class there is greater potential for achieving human understanding or for causing permanent dissension than in almost any other kind of class. Souls are exposed. The chemistry of personalities is a chance factor. I believe in putting the class as a whole before any individual in it and in making the psychological well-being of the kids more important than the quality of their writing.

Even though I started off this essay by being a little flippant and suggesting that I liked being free of literature, the truth is that it's impossible to draw lines between reading and writing in any English course. No matter what the course is called, literature, whether in traditional bound sets or in homemade, photocopied anthologies is at the core of it. I've enjoyed trying to involve students in these choices and in bringing some unexpected examples to them, and I hope that this approach has applications for all teachers.

Just because [your students] are the best and brightest doesn't mean that they really want to learn to write fiction.

10

Nineteen Different Answers and One Black Eye

Todd Strasser

L IKE most of the authors who have contributed chapters to this book, I spend part of each year on the road speaking at junior and senior high schools. In the course of my visits I am asked many questions by students and teachers. Some I have ready answers for, others I don't. But year after year, one of the most perplexing questions I hear is: *How can we teach students to write fiction?*

After nearly twelve years I still have no pat answer. What I do have are bits and pieces of ideas that over time I've managed to string together . . . not into an answer, but rather into an approach to a possible answer.

TALENT AND INSPIRATION

Most of us would probably agree that writing in its simplest form can be taught. You can teach students to create sentences, then to organize those sentences into paragraphs, and to arrange paragraphs logically into an orderly piece of writing. But fiction has to be a lot more than orderly. It has to be interesting.

Some people will argue that fiction does not have to be inter-esting, at least not interesting to anyone other than the writer.

Plenty of people write only for themselves. Take J.D. Salinger. He claims that for the past twenty-five years he's written only for himself and feels no need to publish what he writes. But before that he did happen to publish *Catcher in the Rye*, one of the great landmark pieces of fiction for this century, and a book that still sells hundreds of thousands of copies every year.

Can students be taught not only to write fiction, but also to write interesting fiction? And if so, how? How important is talent? Can that be taught? What about inspiration, the ability to have ideas?

I wish I had hard and fast answers, but I don't. Nor, I suspect, does anyone else. I do have a feeling, though, that talent cannot be learned or acquired to any significant degree. Some people are probably born to be writers, others aren't. But having said that, I also believe that all of us have some amount of talent.

What is talent? Ask twenty people, you'll probably get nineteen different answers, and one black eye. But solely for the purpose of this essay, I would like to propose that talent be thought of as the ability to write fiction that is both readable and interesting. And that to show talent a writer not only must have a smooth and flowing writing style, but also must be capable of having interesting things to say.

Certainly some writers are more readable than others. Judy Blume, Stephen King, and V.C. Andrews are writers teenagers find very readable. You may wish to argue the merits of their writing, but the fact remains that all three have smooth styles of writing and interesting things to say to teens. Regardless of whether you like what they write or not, I would say that all three have a great deal of talent.

What about inspiration? The ability to have ideas for writing fiction? This still seems surprising to me, but unlike talent, I have come to believe that inspiration can be taught. In other words, I'm proposing that students can be taught to have ideas for the fiction they write.

Why do I think this? For years people used to ask me where I got my ideas for books, and did I find it hard to come up with them. I used to be surprised at these questions, since I usually had more ideas for books than time to write them.

It occurred to me one day that without being conscious of it, I had taught myself to have ideas, to look at life in a way that provided me with inspiration. Like most writers I discovered that I get my ideas from conflict, and that my stories are always about how conflict is resolved.

But now for this important interruption:

WHO SHOULD BE TAUGHT?

So far I've brought up a lot of questions, but there's one more that I'd like to address: the question of who should be taught to write fiction and who shouldn't. Too often, it seems, when I do a fiction writing workshop I am presented with a group of students who are said to represent the best and brightest the school has to offer. But just because they're the best and brightest does that mean that they really want to learn to write fiction? Does that mean that they have the most talent and the best ideas?

I've found that sometimes the answer is no. Just because they're the best and brightest doesn't mean they give a hoot about writing fiction. These students tend to be highly motivated and goal oriented, often already on a track to whatever career they've chosen for themselves. And unless their goal is to be a writer, or they like to write as a hobby, these students tend to participate in a fiction writing workshop as if it were any other class. They grasp the concepts quickly, they do quite well in the exercises, but what they've learned will probably lie dormant for the rest of their lives. About the only difference between these kids and *D* students is that you can pretty much expect these kids to be better behaved.

By the way, some writers who approach fiction as a "hobby" have been tremendously successful. Scott Turow, surely one of our widely read and most prosperous novelists, is a full-time lawyer in Chicago. Students who are determined to become novelists and nothing else sometimes worry me. I often ask, once you've learned to write, what do you intend to write about? Having spent the past twelve years as a full-time novelist, I tend to recommend that young writers have a primary career in some other field and write fiction part time. This is partly for financial reasons, but mostly because writers need life experience for material to write about.

Probably the most important single ingredient in learning to write fiction is the desire to write fiction. That's why I generally ask that my writing workshops be attended on a voluntary basis by those students, regardless of their grade average, who most want to learn to write fiction.

QUICK ADVICE

When I am asked by aspiring authors (teachers as often as students) what they should do to become fiction writers (and I mean to include writing for movies and television as well), I generally say the following three things:

1. *Read.* We all know that writing is mostly rewriting, but what really happens when we rewrite? Maybe it's different with other writers, but it seems to me that rewriting means comparing my writing to some standard of literature I maintain in my head. When I hit a spot that isn't up to par, I start to rewrite. Obviously every writer has a different standard. How do we create our own standard of writing? By reading and deciding what writing we like and what writing we don't like. That's why if you want to write, it's especially important to read books (or scripts) in the genre you're trying to write for.

2. *Write.* You wouldn't believe how many people of all ages tell me they want to start writing . . . "just as soon as school's over," or "after I get my master's degree," or "when I go on sabbatical," or "as soon as we move," and on and on. I have a friend who has been working on a novel for twelve years. He's researched it extensively, filled notebooks with notes, outlined chapter by chapter, and he talks about it all the time. But he hasn't written a line of fiction.

3. *Don't let anyone tell you you can't do it.* Everyone's heard the stories about books that were rejected by 120 different publishers, about people who wallpapered their houses with rejection slips. That may all be true, but an even greater truth is that all the newspapers and magazines you see on the newsstands and all the publishers whose books you see in bookstores need material desperately. Television also has an enormous appetite for written material. It takes time and hard work to become a writer, but once you've mastered the craft (which is no easy accomplishment) and familiarized yourself with a field, you will have a good shot at finding work.

There's a fourth, "optional" suggestion that, as far as I'm concerned, becomes more and more mandatory each year:

4. *Learn to write with a word processor.* Certainly scribes were employed after the invention of the printing press, and today many people still write rough drafts by hand, but in this fast-paced ever more productive society of ours, what is the point in doing it the old-fashioned way? If you want to take an hour to craft a single sentence, why not spend that hour crafting it on the word processor? That way when you're ready to turn in the final draft you won't have to retype the entire manuscript. All you'll have to do is press the *print* button.

I don't believe anyone who tells me they save time on creative work with a word processor. It's the "drudge" work where you save time. By the way, it is far easier, and safer, to learn to use a computer than it is to learn to drive. If I had my way, students would be required to learn to use a word processor before they were allowed to take driver's education.

CONFLICT

Back to teaching fiction writing in the classroom. As I mentioned before, I believe that inspiration can be taught. That is, students can be taught to come up with ideas for stories. Not that your students will all come up with the next *Outsiders*, but they should be able to come up with ideas to write about.

Sometimes I'll start a writing workshop by asking the students if they've ever felt like writing, or were told to write, but couldn't come up with an idea? A few hands usually go up and this leads to the first point of the day, which is that in order to have an idea for a story *there must be a conflict.*

A story or novel generally begins with the introduction of a conflict. The student who can't come up with an idea for a story isn't thinking in terms of conflict. Everybody's heard of "Man Versus Man." "Man Versus Nature (or Society)." "Man Versus Himself." I usually go over all three and ask the students to come up with examples of each. This is just to make sure we're on common ground. As far as I know, writers don't sit around wondering what kind of conflict they'll use this week. We just tell stories. For most of us, focusing on the conflict has become second nature.

Sometimes I'll pull the nearest YA novel off the shelf and read the first paragraph and ask the students to identify the conflict. Just now I pulled out Judy Blume's *Are You There God? It's Me, Margaret*:

> Are you there God? It's me, Margaret. We're moving today. I'm so scared God. I've never lived anywhere but here. Suppose I hate my new school? Suppose everybody hates me?

In those seven short sentences are enough conflicts to, well, fill a book. Robert Newton Peck begins *A Day No Pigs Would Die* with: "I should of been in school that day." Which, of course, makes us wonder why he wasn't.

And just so I don't feel left out . . . the beginning of my first novel, *Angel Dust Blues*: "The handcuffs dug into Alex Lazar's wrists." So we know immediately that Alex has been arrested. And we'll want to find out why. And what will happen to Alex next.

When it comes to student writing, the old rule, "Write about what you know," is an important one. You either write about things you've experienced or you research them so well it feels like you've experienced them. Since a writing workshop is about writing and not about researching, I find it best to get the students to write about conflicts they're familiar with.

The most often cited conflicts are "School," "Homework," "Parents," and "Siblings."

But parents alone aren't a conflict. What is the conflict with parents?

"They won't let me stay out late," answers a young lady.

That's conflict: Parents not letting their daughter stay out late. Or parents making their son do his homework. Or the conflict is an older brother or sister picking on the younger one. A conflict can also be a mystery that needs solving, or a challenge that must be overcome. It's anything, really, that creates tension.

THE END

The next step may seem a little premature, but it has proved to be very valuable in my own writing. Once we know the conflict, it's important to have some rough idea of the end. I often prepare the students for this by asking, "How many of you have had a great idea for a story and have started with a huge burst of energy only to find yourself lost after the first page?" The hands go up and now we're ready for the second step.

I know it's called creative writing, and writers do make up a lot as they go along, but without a destination they may never arrive. It is also true that sometimes writers have to write the whole book just to find out what the end will be. The writer Geoffrey Wolff once said that he often has to write the entire first draft of a novel just to find out what the novel is *about*! He then abandons much of the first draft and starts fresh. (Mr. Wolff, while probably one of the finest writers alive today, is not one of the most prolific.)

And that's precisely the rub. It can take months, if not years, to discover the ending if the writer has to write a whole draft of the book first. Since workshops generally last a few hours at most, and since the stories students write tend to be fairly simple, I find it best if the student writers decide on the end before they start.

Going back to the conflict of parents not wanting their daughter to stay out late: What's the end? There are an infinite number of possibilities, and it's up to the students to decide. Whatever end the writer chooses will reflect the personalities of the characters in the story and will give the writer a sense of where to begin.

For instance, if the story will end with some kind of compromise between the parents and the daughter, then the writer knows he or she will have to make the parents and the daughter fairly stubborn but reasonable enough to eventually compromise. If the end is the daughter running away forever, then the writer probably has to make the parents unreasonable people. If the story ends in some sort of calamity for the daughter, then perhaps there is something in her personality that is too unyielding. It really doesn't matter what ending the writer chooses, and it is common for the writer to change the ending several times before even reaching it. But it is still extremely helpful to have an end in mind before starting the story.

SHOW VERSUS TELL

I would guess that most editors will tell you that this is the greatest single difference between publishable work and unpublishable work, between what is interesting to read and what isn't. The student

writer might write, "The sound grew louder and Jack was scared."
The professional writer would choose a different course:

> Jack heard the loud grating sound again. It seemed to come
> from around the corner. It was growing louder, and closer.
> Jack felt his heart begin to race. His palms were moist and his
> mouth, dry. He took a step back, one foot turned slightly as if
> ready to spring into a quick retreat. The sound grew louder
> still. Jack tensed, his breath grew short. Whatever it was, it
> was coming closer . . .

Sometimes a junior- or senior-high student will show me a
"book" he or she has written. It's usually ten to forty pages long,
although some go more than one hundred pages. Almost always,
what the student has written in the first page or two contains enough
for two or three chapters if the writer concentrated on showing and
not on telling.

Writers use words to create pictures, and it has always seemed
to me that the more precise and clear (using detail) those pictures
are, the more interesting the writing is. I think you'll find this true
with nonfiction writing as well.

If the daughter has a fight with the parents over staying out,
show what started the fight and how each character behaves during
the fight. This would almost certainly involve dialogue (I once
heard Richard Peck say that one of the keys to writing for teenagers
is to try to get dialogue on the first printed page) and would also
be the beginning of character development, which will make the
end believable.

So it is important, once the student writer has chosen his or
her conflict, to show it, not just tell it. (In TV writing it's: "Play,
don't say.")

THE STORY

Once the student decides on the conflict, the story becomes: *showing
how the conflict is resolved so that the desired end is achieved.* This is
what keeps the reader reading. Here's a typical discussion between
a class and myself:

"Okay. We've got the conflict. The daughter wants to stay out
late but her parents won't let her. And we've got the end. The girl

and her parents will compromise on a curfew they can all live with. How do we get to that point? After she has the fight with her parents, what happens next?"

"She stays out late anyway."

"And then what?"

"Her parents ground her."

"And then what?"

"The next weekend comes along and her parents won't let her go out so she shoots them."

"Why won't that work for our story?"

"Because it's against the law?"

"This is fiction, you can do whatever you want. But there's a reason why she can't shoot her parents."

"Because it doesn't bring us to the end we agreed on?"

"Right. If she shoots her parents, it becomes a whole different story with a whole different ending. Now, if you want to write that story, fine, but it takes us away from the story we're trying to tell here. So what happens instead?"

"The next weekend comes and she sneaks out."

"And then what happens?"

"Her parents catch her and send her to private school."

"Okay, and then what?"

"She runs away."

"And?"

"Her parents are really worried because they don't know where she is. And maybe they start to realize that at least when she stayed out late they knew where she was."

"And since the end will be a compromise, what's happening to the daughter?"

"She's in a strange town somewhere with no place to stay and she's scared and wishes she was home again."

"Good. Now what?"

"The police find her and bring her home, and she's sure her parents are gonna kill her but instead they're really nice and everyone sits down and comes up with the compromise."

"Great. Just remember to show it, not tell it."

So the way we get to the end of the story is basically by following our own common sense, asking ourselves what the logical steps are that each character has to take to reach the agreed-upon end.

How interesting and readable will this story be? That is where skill and talent come into play. Every writer will handle the story differently, choosing different scenes to show and different words to put into each of the characters' mouths. Some writers have an ear for good dialogue, others have a knack for writing action or emotional scenes. Some of it can be learned. But, as I've said before, I honestly believe that for the most part you're either born with it or you're not.

SOME EXERCISES

Ideally student writers would have weeks to write and polish this story. But they never do. The workshops I conduct are an hour and a half at the most—a woefully inadequate amount of time, usually not enough to show the conflict, much less write the story. So what I often do instead is work on a couple of writing exercises designed to get the students thinking about showing instead of telling.

The first exercise involves description. After reminding the students that we are trying to use words to create pictures, I ask them to imagine either a very hot or a very cold day. I ask them to think about their senses on such a day. What do they see, smell, feel, hear, and taste? (But I also stress that this is not grocery-list writing. It may be that on that particular day they don't taste or hear anything.)

Just before I ask them to describe this day in words, I throw in one last twist—nowhere on their papers can they use the words *hot, cold, boiling, frigid,* or state the temperature. All I want them to do is create a picture so that the reader can see what kind of day it is without being told.

Another exercise involves describing a person in such a way that we learn something about them. Without using such words as *rich* or *poor, happy* or *sad,* I ask the students to describe a character who would fit those terms. Sometimes the student writers decide to describe some other kinds of characters, but again without attaching a label to them. In recent years students have created some startling depictions of priests, drunks, hookers . . . and school principals.

The third and final exercise (and often the one the students have the most fun with) involves dialogue. First I go over some basic guidelines: Whatever is said is put in quotes. A new paragraph is started each time a different character speaks. Is it important to identify the speaker. Stick to verbs like *said, yelled, answered,* and *asked* while avoiding words like *declared, announced,* and *proclaimed.* (For each of these guidelines I can probably find a novel that is a brilliantly written exception. But we're talking fundamentals here.)

I also talk about the usefulness of attaching an action to the dialogue where it is necessary or desired. For instance, *"I'll always love you,"* he said, pulling the trigger means something quite different from *"I'll always love you,"* he said, pulling the blinds.

There's also the character's interior monologue: *"It's wonderful to see you again,"* I said, wondering how in the world I would escape from him this time.

THE END (FOR REAL)

My best subjects in high school were math and science. I was a horrible speller (thank God for computer programs that check spelling), and on two separate occasions I was sent to reading tutors because I was reading below grade level. My reading comprehension was, and probably still is, terrible, and I was never able to memorize a speech from Shakespeare.

How did I become a fiction writer? Mostly by trial and error, and by a tremendous need and desire to write. And that leads me to say that, yes, fiction writing can be taught to some degree, but I think that those who truly have a burning desire to write will find a way whether they attend class or not.

Writing is a process that can be improved by work.

11

Writing, Rewriting, Rejection, and Recognition
Some Lessons from a Writer's Workshop

Walter Dean Myers

WHEN the writing process is formalized into theory it invariably puts some distance between the artist and the art. When the artists are already on the fringe of the larger society, as is the case with many under-privileged youngsters, that distance can be overwhelming. Theory is also less important to the development of a writer than regular work. Writers write. If young people can be brought to the habit of regular production, they can become successful. By successful I mean the ability to produce material that some publication will at least seriously consider.

Public School 40 in Jersey City, N.J., is a school that draws its student body from a mixed neighborhood of private homes and high-rise projects. In the summer of 1988 I was asked by a teacher, Jim Aumack, to come to the school and speak to the kids. As a result of my visit to the school and conversations with Aumack I began a writing workshop that fall that has continued until now. The kids in the workshop have all expressed an interest in writing and many have seen the magazine from the previous year's workshop that the kids and I publish each June. The children vary each year—sometimes I have more seventh- and eighth-graders, some-times more sixth-graders—so the first few weeks of each year be-come a feeling-out process. The approach varies with the skills the children bring, but I stick to the same basic ideas.

One of the first things I do is to bring in a manuscript fresh from the editor with all of the editorial notes still attached. I have written on the board that writing is a three-step process: thinking, writing, and rewriting. Explaining that I am currently engaged in the rewriting process, I start going over the editor's comments, asking my students to consider them with me. Shall I make the suggested change? Is the material really "not clear" as the editor has suggested? One student, noting all the blue slips on *Fallen Angels*, was close to tears. My explanation that the slips were op-portunities to improve the work (if I agreed with the editor's com-ments) did not impress the student.

The students accept some of the editorial changes suggested, argue about others, and discuss the role of the editor. What they get from the procedure is the idea that writing is a process that can be improved by work. Many children who have been told that they had "writing talent" or are "gifted" seem to feel ill at ease with this concept. To them "gifted" means that they don't have to work at writ-ing. Most, however, see that the final drafts of my work are better than the first and soon understand that it is the job of the writer to bring the work to the highest level of skill he or she may possess.

One young writer, seeing all the drafts, the editorial changes a manuscript went through, asked what made me special if I have to do so much work.

"I do the work," I told her.

My prestige wasn't increased when I began to show the young people some of the devices that I use to make writing easier. The first one I showed them was a job application from a local company.

Since I find character the major consideration in preparing a book, I ask my writers to fill out job applications for one character they wish to write about. They are therefore thinking about the character before writing, making decisions about the character's appearance, background, experience, etc. I then show them a form that I use, a modified job application with more detailed infor-mation.

For all the writers, but especially those who are writing poetry, I offer my ECLAIR formula:

E — Emotion
C — Clarity
L — Language that Sings
A — Argument
I — Imagination
R — Rhythm

By argument I mean that the writer wants to sway the reader toward a specific point of view. Argument has a utility that, in my view, meaning lacks.

When we begin criticizing material, the ECLAIR formula is somewhere in sight, and critical comments are directed toward the concepts in the formula.

We do simple plotting, starting with a personality trait of a character and seeing how that character reacts to some crisis. We plot the crisis on a time line.

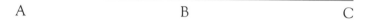

A   B   C

The interaction between character and event starts at point A. They reach a crisis at point B, which is where we begin the story. We incorporate the important events from section A—B in the story (hopefully without resorting to flashbacks) and show why the crisis had to happen and how B—C is a natural result of A—B. (Flashbacks are sometimes useful, but by looking for ways of not using them the child is doing the work of thinking like a writer.)

Usually I demonstrate how I've done this or how some other writer has accomplished it. My early drafts are particularly useful here when the plotting goes off course. There's no problem in telling the children that the editor sometimes suggests my final direction. The most rewarding session is when, after I've discussed a problem, someone in the class comes up with a great solution.

Before each class I usually tell the young writers what I've been doing the week before. Has someone offered me a contract? Is some editor being unreasonable? Who did I see at the ALA meeting? Then we read from material they previously turned in, emphasizing that we are looking for ways to improve it, that it is not yet a finished piece. The work that is completed over the year is published in our anthology.

"Laundry lists" are useful. Taking the applications we have filled out earlier, we make a list of characteristics. *John is tall, thin, dark haired, Latino, 14, and slope shouldered.* We work on ways of saying these things without making it sound like a list, trying to avoid sentences such as:

> John, the tall, dark haired boy looked into the mirror and saw how thin he was. "I hope I'm not this thin next year when I'm 15," he said in Spanish.

This exercise is always amusing as the kids try unsuccessfully to sneak lists of adjectives past each other.

I make a big deal of the instance, and I think it is a big deal, when a rewrite involves only a minor improvement or when the writer is not sure if it is an improvement. We read the material aloud, then read it silently, to see which way is truer to the writer's voice and meaning.

There are no restrictions on subject matter, but I try to be sensitive to the students. These young people are often from difficult backgrounds. Sometimes there are stories involving sexual abuse, drugs, or family violence. Are they writing from a personal experience that needs to be brought to someone's attention? Should the piece be read aloud? It's a judgment call.

I encourage the students to send their material to outside magazines such as *Shoe Tree* and *Merlyn's Pen*, and we've had a few successes. One of my worries was that the kids would be upset about being rejected, so I brought in some of my rejection slips and letters. Most of the rejection slips they received were accepted graciously. They would rather have had acceptances but they enjoyed getting the mail, and most children's publications write gentle rejection slips, if there can be such a thing as a gentle rejection slip. I wrote an eighty-page western/adventure story that was recently rejected by several houses and they seemed delighted. I'll have to give a class in compassion.

Sometimes we read from published books, especially badly written books. The kids and I rewrite pages from these books or replot them and try to figure out why the publisher bothered with them. Often we can't.

By the time May rolls around and Mr. Aumack and I are calling for last changes in manuscripts, yelling at kids about deadlines, and trying to decide on format, there's usually a healthy disrespect for the art of writing and considerably more respect for the work of writing. My group knows more about me (they're all sworn to secrecy) than anybody except my psychiatrist. They know how much money I make because they've seen all the contracts, looked at the royalty statements so they understand the business of being a writer, and agonized with me over my next proposal.

They express everything from annoyance to delight at my editors, sometimes suggesting particularly unkind remarks for me to pass along. Sometimes I do pass them along, but I also show the writers when the editors are correct in their judgment, and note when I've changed my mind about an editor's comments.

If we have children who can draw, we ask them to illustrate the stories. The illustrators usually work apart from the writers and there's the usual griping (She calls *that* art?) but the final result is usually well received. I know the children are proud of their achievements because it represents a major effort on their part to get the work ready for publication. The work is uneven, a necessity given the population I'm working with, but that's okay, too. I've never been prouder to work with a group than my P.S. 40 writers.

My workshop sessions, usually two a month, are scheduled around my own writing activities. A classroom teacher works with me and is available to the children during the regular school time. Bringing in an outside writer is not the answer to improving all writing skills, but it can make a difference for students to see how the work is done in "real life."

When children have read, or have had read to them, at least one of the author's books, an emotional connection is made between the students and the speaker.

12

Secrets to Successful Author Visits

Gloria D. Miklowitz

"WHY," I asked Virginia Beane during school visits in Fort Worth, Texas, "spend so much money on an author visit when the money could go to buy badly needed books?" Virginia had just explained that she only had a book budget of four dollars per student each year for her library. And that had to cover AV and other equipment needs, as well.

The sum she was allowed with which to purchase new books was paltry, indeed. I felt embarrassed at the cost of my visit—the honorarium, fare, and expenses—and guilty that I might be depriving students of much-needed books.

Not to worry, she said. Author-visit funds came from other sources, principally grants. You could buy all the books in the world, but getting kids to read them was another matter. Author visits resulted in a strong increase in demand for books, especially those of the author.

I heard much the same from Sherry Fukuhara, in Castroville, California. "Before Michael French spoke at our school, only boys read his book *Pursuit*. Now, both sexes read it."

Pearl Goodwin of Littleton, Colorado, spoke of the effect of author visits on nonreaders. After my talk at Columbine High, she told me that several boys who'd never borrowed books from the library before asked to check out my *After the Bomb*. And when they'd read that, they wanted its sequel, *After the Bomb, Week One*. "It's such a joy to turn nonreaders into readers," she said.

It's flattering, of course, to know that author talks turn kids on to books. But there's much more they gain. When I tell students that I don't wait for inspiration but sit down every day for four or five hours, whether or not the ideas are flowing, they learn that talent isn't enough. Writing a book, like achieving *anything* of value in life, involves hard work and immense amounts of discipline.

When I show students a typical manuscript page with all its cut-and-paste inserts and editing, they go back to their own writing with a different attitude. And when they ask about "writer's block" and I say you work your way through it by more research, more trial and error, and never by giving up, they understand the difference between the professional writer and the novice.

For those who have had authors to their schools there's no need to go on about its advantages. But for those who have not, or who have arranged such visits but wonder if they could have worked better, here are some suggestions.

CHOOSING AN AUTHOR

Each author has his or her own style. Not all are good speakers, or good with children. The best authors give a clear picture of the entire writing and publishing process—from where the ideas begin, through research and development of characters, to editing and publishing problems.

Ask other librarians which authors they've heard who give good presentations and interact well with students. When you attend professional meetings try to go to at least some author sessions to get a sense of different styles. How do speakers relate to the audience? Are they merely entertaining, but lacking substance? Do they use the time to read from their work, rather than tell how it came about?

CONTACTING THE AUTHOR

The best way to reach an author is through the public relations office of his or her principal publisher, or the publisher of the book your students are studying by that author.

The PR person can give you an idea of the author's availability, customary fee, and special requirements (how many talks the author can handle a day, to what age and size audience, whether he or she prefers staying at a hotel or private accommodation, for example). This representative can send you promotional materials and some-times free books and can facilitate the ordering of books at discount.

The PR person is the liaison between author and school, es-pecially in the first stages where fees are discussed. After these initial arrangements have been made you may want to speak directly with the author, whose address and phone number can be obtained from the PR person.

Another way to reach an author is by a bit of sleuthing. The flap copy on hardcovers often tells the city and state where the writer lives. Consult the phone book. If the number is listed, the address probably will be, too. In addition, you can often find where authors live from reference books such as *Who's Who in America, Who's Who of American Women* and *Something About the Author.* Write the author, or phone. More can be accomplished quickly by phone but some writers prefer not to be disturbed while working and will return your call left on an answering machine. Fees are best discussed with the PR person at the publisher's, unless your honorarium is not open for negotiation.

PLANNING WITH THE AUTHOR

Once you have established that this is the speaker you want and that he or she is available, you'll want to put in writing what the conditions of the visit are: the date, number of presentations, grade level of students to be addressed, fee and exactly what expenses are covered. You will want to discuss which books to order for auto-graphing, and for reading in school before the visit. (Some books may be out of print. Check *Books in Print* or ask the author.) Will a projector be needed? What flight will the author arrive on? How will you recognize each other? (Have the host hold up a copy of the author's book at the agreed meeting place.) Do you plan to go to dinner after the author's arrival? If possible, tell the author where he or she will be booked in the event of a mix-up at the airport.

If the author lives nearby and is driving, provide a good map showing how to reach your school and send it well in advance of the visit.

FINANCING THE VISIT

Before you can invite an author you need to know how much it will cost (the publishing company's PR spokesperson can give you this information), and that funds will be available.

Author fees vary and are somewhat negotiable. They range from around $300 a day up to $1500 or perhaps more, plus expenses. If these charges are too steep, consider inviting a local author or one whose name is not yet well known. Perhaps the local children's librarian or bookstore could suggest someone. Even then an honorarium is in order.

Unless the author is local or from the same state the cost of travel can be considerable. Oddly, coast-to-coast airfare often costs less than importing an author from the next state. Recently, by staying over Saturday night, I saved my hosts $600 in fare. If your author can do that, be prepared to spend at least part of Saturday with him or her, showing the sights.

Hotel and food costs need not be great. Most authors don't expect or require the most expensive digs; they're not in their rooms that much. But ask. While one may prefer staying in a private home, another might want a suite at the Plaza. Most, however, are happy with a quiet, clean, and safe room where, after the long day, they can close their overworked mouths, put up their tired feet, and relax.

Once you have an idea of what it will cost to bring the author, it's time to ferret out the funds. Some librarians apply for grants, often as much as a year before the author is invited. Some hold book fairs, usually in early December for holiday gift giving. Your book supplier or local bookstore should offer a good discount and will take back unsold books. For schools with an active PTA, funds raised by the organization may be earmarked for author visits. Reminder: When getting books from the publisher for autographing, the discount is usually 40 percent.

Just a few words about payment: Often, when an author speaks at several schools in the same area over a period of days, the payment comes from more than one source. Each school should be responsible for its share (including travel and expenses), and paperwork should be drawn up and signed months before. Although travel reimbursement may be sent later, payment for talks should be made the day the author speaks. It's uncomfortable for an author to have to write months after a visit about the check that hasn't yet come.

It's just as uncomfortable for the librarian to find that the delay was due to some form that hadn't been signed.

TIMING THE VISIT

It's a good idea to line up an author at least six months before the visit for three reasons.

1. The author you want may already be booked and you will need to find someone else. Most schools schedule far in advance. October, November, and February through May are the busiest months for author visits.

2. You need time to prepare your school—not only the students, but also the teachers—for the author's appearance.

3. The book-ordering process and paperwork to bring the author often takes weeks to get through the school district and months more to get through the publisher. Once the books arrive at the school it takes time for the students to read them before the author's visit.

If books are ordered for autographing, be sure to check the order when it arrives. More than one librarian has opened that first box of books on the morning of the author's visit to find someone else's titles inside. Just as bad is the order that arrives the day after the author has left.

One of my fondest memories of a school visit illustrates the value of early preparation. Some years ago when I was writing principally for the grade school child, I was invited a year in advance to speak as "Author of the Year" at Taft Elementary School in Taft, California.

During the year the entire school became involved in my anticipated appearance. Children read my books or, if unable to read yet, had my books read to them. They wrote their own stories about animals (because some of my first books were about animals), and these stories were posted with pride in the hallways of the school. The PTA and older students constructed three-dimensional, life-size, papier-mâché zoo animals and placed them in the school entry. In the cafeteria I found a replica of the haunted house on the cover of my Scholastic book *Ghastly Ghostly Riddles* and a huge, colorful banner welcoming me.

At the luncheon planned by the PTA mothers I cut a cake in the shape of a book, decorated as *The Zoo That Moved*. And finally, I was presented with a huge quilt planned and sewn by PTA members. Every other square of the quilt, on both sides, was a child-drawn picture representing one of my first books: *Barefoot Boy; The Zoo That Moved; Harry Truman; Sad Song, Happy Song; Ghastly Ghostly Riddles*; etc. Preparations for my visit *had* to have begun many months before. I could not have felt more welcome, nor more honored than at that school.

PREPARING THE SCHOOL

Have multiple copies of the author's books on hand in the library long before the visit. If possible, order classroom paperback sets of a title so English classes can read and discuss the book. Alert your public library and children's bookstore of the anticipated visit so they may stock extra books.

I have always felt embarrassed when I speak at a school where the children haven't heard of me until the moment of introduction. I feel insulted that the teachers haven't prepared the school. Authors are not there to entertain. They come to share with the students how they do what they do. When children have read, or have had read to them, at least one of the author's books, an emotional connection is made between the students and the speaker.

If any of the author's books have been made into school-break or after-school television specials, try to acquire a copy so the students may see the video and compare it with the book. It's one of the best ways to develop critical skills.

Promotional materials from the publisher (author brochures, photos, book jackets) can be displayed in the library so students can see what the author looks like and become familiar with his or her background.

ARRANGING THE AUTHOR'S SCHEDULE

Some authors prefer to speak only once; others will handle as many as four presentations a day. I find three presentations as much as I can manage, especially when the day often involves lunch with teachers and librarians, autographing, interviews with the local press and private time with special students interested in writing or needing to confide about their problems. Returning home after three or four days "on" in schools is enough to exhaust me for a week. I also like to have a copy of the day's schedule. It helps me ration my energy.

Most schools want the author to speak to large groups in order to expose as many children as possible to the speaker and to justify the expense. Crowded auditoriums, where the author can't make eye contact with each child, are the least favorite places to speak. It's disconcerting to note a teacher admonishing a kid in the back when the author can't even see that child's face. Most authors prefer small groups in classroom or library settings, so there is opportunity for an exchange of ideas. Why not have at least one of the three or four sessions in a day given to the really interested writing students?

Speaking tours are killing days. If the author is from the West Coast and speaking the next day on the East Coast at 8:30 in the morning, that's 5:30 A.M. western mental time. The first day, if possible, schedule the first talk a bit later if the author comes from another time zone. Have plenty of coffee available. Make clear when each period starts and ends so the speaker can budget time. Have a microphone available, if needed, and test it before the talk.

Introducing the Author. Often the librarian or a teacher briefly introduces the author, but I've been at schools where a student has been given that honor. While the better organized introduction may come from the adults, student introductions make the day more "theirs." It brings audience and author closer. The honor can be given to the kid who has read the most books, or written a meaningful paper on a book. With only a forty-five- to fifty-minute time slot, the introduction should be short so there's time for questions at the end of the session.

Videotaping. Don't videotape without the author's permission. Some people are rattled by a camera pointing at them and distrust how they might photograph. Also, if a video is made, the author has the right to know just where it will be shown. The same courtesy applies to audio taping.

Asking Questions of the Author. This is an important part of an author visit, and there are many ways to handle it. First, the author can call for questions after the talk. One disadvantage is that the first question may not come readily. It takes one spunky kid to start the ball rolling before others will follow with questions. Another disadvantage is inaudibility. The questioner is often shy and remains seated. His or her words must be repeated and passed forward before the author can hear them. That wastes time.

A successful way to initiate questions is to have a brief break after the talk so questions may be written on cards and handed to the author. The disadvantage here is screening and duplication of questions.

The very best method for questions is for each teacher whose class will attend the author's presentation to discuss what the class would most like to ask. Appoint one student to present that class's questions. After the author's talk, the representatives from each class may line up at a microphone. Each student asks one question, waits for the answer, then goes to the back of the line until his or her turn comes again.

The advantage to this method is that the questions can be well thought out in advance. The speaker as well as the audience can hear each question clearly. More questions can be answered because of the rapid-fire delivery.

Autographing. A school period, perhaps lunchtime, should be set aside for book autographing. The library is a good place for selling the books (before the visit and after the talk). I like to feel unrushed enough to be able to look at each student and perhaps share a few words. Signing scraps of paper is my least favorite occupation. I suspect the paper finds its way into the wastebasket before the student even leaves school.

FOLLOWING UP

A letter to the author from the teacher or librarian who initiated the visit, with a copy to the PR person at the publishing house, is always welcome. If photos were taken, or an article has appeared in the school or local newspaper, it's appreciated when copies are enclosed.

After the author's visit, be prepared for an onslaught of requests for the visitor's books. I've been told that interest in that author goes on for years at a school, passed on by word of mouth to new students.

Students may want to write the author to ask additional questions or to convey their reactions to what they've read. I've frequently given out my address to students passionately anxious to communicate with me. If letters are sent to the author, remind the writer to include a self-addressed stamped envelope. Authors get hundreds of letters a year from readers. The ones I answer first are those with SASE's.

Some teachers like to make a class project of writing to the author after a visit. I always read each student's letter but respond with a single answer to the whole class, trying to cover most of the questions asked. The sequel to *After the Bomb* might never have been written had it not been for the urging of readers. Thousands of junior and senior high students wrote telling me what they still wanted to know—which became the basis for *After the Bomb, Week One.*

BENEFITS TO THE AUTHOR

Speaking at schools and conferences throughout the U.S. and in other countries, I have gained as much as I've given. I've met and become friends with some of the most wonderful and caring librarians and teachers in the world. I've been able to touch many of the young people who are my readers, and have established a bond of love and trust with them.

Author visits should be an important part of every school program. The good fallout goes on for years.